101

Squirrel

Hunting

Tips

(& a few ways to cook 'em)

101 Squirrel Hunting Tips

(& a few ways to cook 'em)

Dennis Trisler

101 Squirrel Hunting Tips (& A Few Ways to Cook 'em)

© 2003 by Dennis Trisler

Revised 2013

Disclaimer: The author and publisher disclaim all liability in connection with the use of 101 Squirrel Hunting Tips. It is intended only as an informative guide for those seeking information about squirrel hunting and recipes featuring squirrel meat as the primary ingredient. Our recommendations are based on experience and data from sources we believe to be reliable. Accordingly, the reader must take responsibility for decisions and actions regarding his or her choice to implement or practice any idea, suggestion, recommendation, instruction, or advice in this book.

The information offered herein is general and is made without guarantees by either the author or publisher.

Contents

Cooking Squirrels 91

Squirrel Recipes 93

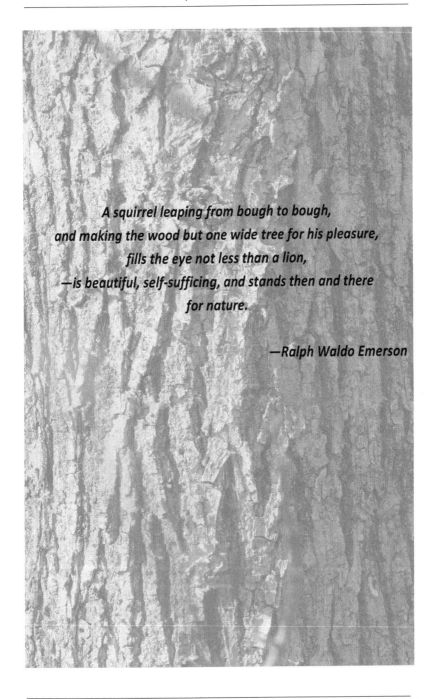

*A squirrel leaping from bough to bough,
and making the wood but one wide tree for his pleasure,
fills the eye not less than a lion,
—is beautiful, self-sufficing, and stands then and there
for nature.*

—Ralph Waldo Emerson

Introduction

Many of us were introduced to the sport and art of hunting when we were young, by first learning to hunt squirrels.

I was about ten when my father took me squirrel hunting for the first time. We didn't go far that morning, venturing only a few yards into the thick woods behind the house. The shaggy barked hickories, the brawny gray-skinned beeches, the towering oaks that grew on the hillside just outside our back door, all heavily laden with nuts and acorns, attracted a lot of fox and gray squirrels. And since the squirrels were plentiful and close, we didn't have to walk too far or climb too high to find them. We didn't actually have to *hunt* for them.

Which was more than okay with my dad. He liked to hunt, and he especially liked to hunt squirrels, even though he was not what I consider a diehard hunter...but he never cared much for unnecessary exertion.

And it was okay with me, too. I was just thrilled to be out in autumn woods with my dad, just the two of us together, just him and me, father and son... hunting.

Well, he was doing the hunting, and the shooting; I was watching, listening and learning.

During that first hunt, and during our later hunts together, I learned from his whispered instructions how to carry a gun in the woods—cradled like a baby in the crook of my left arm. I learned how to load a gun and unload it, how to tell when it was 'on safe' and how and when to take the safety off. I learned how to aim and *squeeeeeze* the trigger.

I learned to respect a gun's destructive power, and I learned that responsibility is an indispensable part of owning and using a firearm. I learned never to point a gun, even a gun that I knew was not loaded, at anyone or anything I did not intend to shoot. "More people have been killed with unloaded guns than with loaded guns," Dad told me on more than one occasion. Which I knew couldn't possibly be true. But, also knowing Dad's propensity for using exaggeration to make a point, I recognized that the basic lesson—treat every gun as if it were loaded—was valid, and it's stuck with me all these years.

I learned how to watch where I stepped even as I watched for movement in the trees. I learned how to listen and understand what I heard, how to stalk and how to stand. I learned patience, persistence and perseverance. And, after getting slapped in the face by briar canes and the springy limbs of saplings a few times, I learned not to follow too closely behind my dad as we made our way through the woods.

I learned all of that, and more....

And the skills and knowledge that I gained during those early squirrel hunts—which I practiced and refined after getting my first 'squirrel rifle' and began hunting on my own—came in handy later when I moved on to other kinds of hunting.

Over the years, I've hunted ducks and geese, rabbits and deer. But it is squirrel hunting that I have always enjoyed most.

Hence this modest book, which offers tested and proven methods for taking squirrels, a little friendly advice, a few lessons learned and tricks of the sport, and even some recipes for turning your squirrel harvests into delicious meals.

Whether you are an experienced squirrel hunter or a youngster just getting started, these 'tips' will enhance your knowledge of squirrels, in general, and squirrel hunting, in particular, to make you a better, safer, and more successful hunter.

•••

About squirrels

Squirrels are rodents.

In scientific terminology, they are members of the Rodentia order of Mammals, which also includes rats and mice and marmots and woodchucks. Rodents have one primary physical trait in common — their teeth are highly specialized for gnawing. In fact, the word 'rodent' is derived from the Latin word *rodere*, which means 'to gnaw.' All rodents, squirrels included, have a single pair of upper incisors and a single pair of lower incisors, which are rootless and never stop growing. Gnawing keeps these teeth ground down and sharpened like tiny chisels.

The squirrel's common name comes from the Greek word *skiouros* — *skia,* which means shade, and *oura,* which means tail — interpreted as 'shade tail' or 'he who sits in the shadow of his tail.' The word 'squirrel' itself is directly derived from the French word *esquirel.* Latinized, the family name for squirrels is *scurinae.*

Worldwide, more than 365 species of squirrels have been classified and divided into seven families. The three most common squirrel families, however, are the ground squirrel, the flying squirrel and the arboreal or tree squirrel.

With the exception of a few species of woodchucks (or ground hogs) and prairie dogs, which are favorites of long-range varmint shooters, ground squirrels generally are not hunted. Neither are flying squirrels, which are nocturnal and not considered a game animal. Flying squirrels also are on the endangered species list and are protected by law.

We hunt tree squirrels.

Several kinds of tree squirrels inhabit North America, but only a few species with a wide range over the United States and Canada are regularly hunted for food and sport. These are mainly the eastern gray squirrel, the western gray squirrel, the fox squirrel, and, to a much lesser extent, the red squirrel.

Tree squirrel characteristics

Tree squirrels, regardless of species, share a number of common physical and behavioral characteristics in addition to the dental structure that marks them as rodents.

All tree squirrels have four sets of whiskers: above and below the eyes, on the nose and underneath the head on the front of the throat. These whiskers, called *vibrissae,* serve as touch receptors and provide the squirrel with information about its immediate surroundings. This is particularly useful when it is inside a dark nest or tree cavity.

They all have a very strong jaw structure, which makes it possible for them to crack open even the hardest nutshells and gnaw through tree bark and tree limbs. They have extremely good eyesight and a wide field of vision, as well as a keen sense of smell and acute hearing.

With their tough curved claws and powerful hind legs tree squirrels are highly adapted to climbing; they can leap almost unbelievable distances and even hang upside down when necessary to reach a particularly desirable nut or acorn or pine cone. Their agility is further complemented by their unique ability to rotate their hind feet 180 degrees, which allows them to descend headfirst. They use their bushy tails for balance and steering when running and jumping.

There is no difference by size or coloration between males and females; however, it's easy to tell which is which during breeding seasons—the female is the one being chased and fought over by five or ten or more males trying to establish dominance. The female mates first with the dominant male; but, later, she will also mate with several other males.

Reproduction for all species is similar, although there are some slight differences.

The gestation period for gray squirrels and fox squirrels is about 45 days; for red squirrels, it is 35 to 38 days. Compared to many other rodents, tree squirrels develop slowly. Newborns are tiny, weighing only about half an ounce, regardless of species. They are completely hairless and blind and totally dependent on their mothers. Their eyes open when they are about four weeks old, and their ears open at about three weeks for red squirrels and six weeks for grays and fox squirrels. Weaning begins at about six or seven weeks and is usually complete at 10 weeks. After about 12 weeks the juveniles will be nearly adult size and independent of their mother. The male juveniles will then leave the nest area and disperse to find their own territory. Juvenile females, however, generally stay close to their birthplace. In eight or nine months the squirrels reach their full adult size.

Tree squirrels do not hibernate. They are active year round during the daytime, even in harsh winter weather. But their activity is greatest from late spring to fall when they feed heavily and store food for the winter months. Activity is also bimodal, i.e., it peaks twice during the day, about two hours after dawn and again late in the afternoon.

Some squirrels have lived 18 to 20 years in captivity; but their life span in the wild is estimated to be only about seven or eight years.

Eastern gray squirrel

Eastern gray squirrels, *Sciurus carolinensis,* including five subspecies, are found throughout the eastern U.S. from Florida to Canada and from the Atlantic coast west to where the deciduous, or hardwood, forests meet the Great Plains. Considered medium size tree squirrels, adult eastern gray squirrels are 15 to 20 inches long and have an 8- to 10-inch tail. They can weigh from 12 to 26 ounces, but their average weight is about a pound. Their fur is dark gray to pale gray across the back and may be tinted reddish on the hips, feet and head. Their tail and belly is white to pale gray, and the tail hairs are generally darker in the middle with white hairs at the tip. Some regional varieties of eastern gray squirrels have coats of uniform color, such as white, gray or black.

Eastern gray squirrels feed primarily on nuts--walnuts, beechnuts, hickory nuts, pecans and acorns are favorite fare—but their generalist diet also includes the fruits, seeds, buds or flowers of maple, mulberry, hackberry, elm, buckeye, horse chestnut, wild cherry, dogwood, hawthorn, and hazelnut, other seeds, berries, fungi, and flowers, and sometimes insects, bird eggs and the inner bark of some trees. They gather and store nuts and acorns to be eaten during the winter when food may not be available by scatter hoarding, i.e., burying individual nuts and acorns in shallow holes around their territory after marking them with their scent. In the winter they use their sharp sense of smell and memory to locate nuts that they cached earlier in the late summer and fall.

Although gray squirrels have adapted well — some might say *too well* — to urban and suburban settings, where they are often considered vermin because of the damage they can do to dwellings, typical eastern gray squirrel habitat is continuous woodland dominated by mature mast-producing trees, such as hickory, oak, and beech, with dense undergrowth.

Mast trees provide not only a primary food source for the squirrels but also places to build nests, called dreys, and dens. Eastern gray squirrels typically use three different types of nesting places: summer dreys, winter dreys, and tree dens.

Dreys are round constructions of interwoven twigs and leaves lined with moss, bark, leaves, fur, feathers, lichen or other soft material. Summer dreys are usually very simple nests, often no more than a flat, saucer shaped platform of leaves and twigs on an exposed branch or in the crotch of a tree. Winter dreys are more elaborate and more permanent and waterproof. Tree dens are holes or cavities in the main trunks of usually deciduous trees, which the squirrels line with soft, warm material in the same way that they line their nests. Eastern grays often use dens in the winter months and dreys in the summer.

Eastern gray squirrels have two breeding seasons a

year—December to February and May to early July The average litter size is three; the winter litter is usually smaller than the summer litter.

Males become sexually mature at 15 to 18 months. Females can reproduce at 10 or 11 months, although most do not breed until they are about 15 months old, and only females more than two years old will breed in both of the seasons and produce two litters per year.

Eastern gray squirrels are not territorial; they have overlapping home ranges that vary in size from one or two acres to more than 50 acres. Male gray squirrels' home range is slightly larger than the females' because of breeding seasons, and ranges increase slightly in the spring and summer for both sexes. The squirrels will also extend their territory to compensate for a scarcity of food or an increase in squirrel population in their normal range.

Western gray squirrel

Western gray squirrels, *Sciurus griseus,* also called California Grey Squirrels, are the only large gray tree squirrels in their range on the west coast of the United States and Canada. In the U.S. their range extends from southern California north into British Columbia. The western gray squirrel shares a number of characteristics with its eastern cousin, but there are some differences.

One difference is their size: At 18 to 24 inches long with a 10- to 12-inch tail and a body weight of 12 ounces to two pounds, western gray squirrels are slightly larger than eastern grays. Coloration is also different. Western grays have gray backs with a lot of white-tipped hairs and a white belly. The backs of their ears are reddish-brown, and their long bushy tails are banded with grayish white and black fur, especially underneath.

Western gray squirrels also have both a summer and winter coat. The spring molt begins in May or June, and the autumn molt begins in September, but the tail molts only once a year during the summer.

Unlike the eastern grays, the western species have only one breeding season a year, which occurs between March and June, and, therefore, have only one litter of newborns a year. Litter size ranges from three to five.

Western gray squirrels are non-territorial, but their home range is usually smaller than the eastern grays', varying in size from about one acre to 17 acres.

They are also scatter hoarders and generalist feeders, but their diet consists primarily of pinecones, acorns, nuts, fungi, berries and sometimes insects.

Western gray squirrels typically use dreys in the summer, which are built in the upper one-third of the tree canopy. In winter, they often prefer to use dens inside hollow trees.

Fox squirrel

Sometimes called Sherman's fox squirrel, mangrove fox squirrel, cat squirrel, or stump-eared squirrel, the fox squirrel, *Sciurus niger*, is the largest tree squirrel in the United States. Its range extends from Florida to Canada and west to the Dakotas, eastern Colorado and Texas. It is not, however, found in New England.

Fox squirrels have three different color phases, depending on their range: In the northeastern part of the their range they have a gray back with a yellowish belly;

in the western part of their range they are almost uniformly reddish in color; in the south they are often black with white on their face and a white-tipped tail. And, in some areas of South Carolina, they have white ears.

They are about 20 percent larger than western gray squirrels. Adult fox squirrels are 18 to 28 inches long with an 8- to 13-inch tail and weigh from 1-1/2 to 3 pounds.

Like the western gray squirrel, fox squirrels have a summer and winter coat. The spring molt begins in March and the autumn molt begins in September. The tail molts once a year, in the summer.

They have two breeding seasons a year — December to February and May to June. Litter size ranges from two to four, and the summer litter is usually larger than the winter litter.

Fox squirrels have large overlapping ranges. They are usually found in forest dominated by oaks and hickories, but in the southern part of their range they inhabit live oak and mixed forest, cypress and mangrove swamps, and piney areas. They are generalist feeders but relish acorns and the nuts, flowers and buds of walnut, hickory and pecan trees. They also eat the fruits, seeds, buds or flowers of maples, mulberry, hackberry, elms, buckeyes, horse chestnuts, wild cherries, dogwoods, hawthorn, hazelnut, and gingko. They will eat pine seeds and the pollen cones of cedar, hemlock, pine and spruce. In summer, they will also eat fungi; in the late fall and winter, they like cultivated crops such as field corn. Animal food items include bones, bird eggs, nestlings and frogs.

They are scatter hoarders like their cousins, the eastern and western gray squirrels. And, like the western grays, they build winter dreys and summer dreys in the upper one-third of tall trees and use dens in cavities in the main trunks of deciduous trees.

They are scatter hoarders like their cousins, the eastern and western gray squirrels. And, like the western grays, they build winter dreys and summer dreys in the upper one-third of tall trees and use dens in cavities in the main trunks of deciduous trees.

Red squirrel

The red squirrel, *Tamiasciurus budsonicus,* also called the pine squirrel or chickaree, inhabits much of Canada and Alaska. In the continental U.S. its range extends throughout the Rocky Mountains and in the northeast from Maine to Virginia.

Red squirrels are much smaller than gray squirrels and fox squirrels, measuring only about 10-1/2 to 15 inches in length with a 3-1/2- to 6-1/2-inch tail and weighing between five and nine ounces.

They are reddish-brown to reddish-gray on their back and white or grayish-white on their belly, with a black line running laterally down their sides. They have both a summer and a winter coat and molt twice a year, in May or June and again in September. The tail molts once a year in the summer.

Red squirrels typically have only one litter per year; breeding takes place from February to March. Sometimes, however, a second litter is produced in August or September. Litter size is three to seven. Unlike fox squirrels and gray squirrels, red squirrels are territorial. Their territories are typically small, only about 2-1/2 to 4 acres. They prefer forest areas ranging from deciduous to coniferous or a mixture of the two types of trees.

They feed primarily on pine seeds, but they also eat acorns and beechnuts, the seeds of hickory, tulip, sycamore, maple and elm, and berries, fungi, insects, bird eggs and even young birds. In the fall they bury pinecones, acorns and other nuts in one place, rather than scatter them throughout their territory. This is called larder hoarding, and their storage area is called a midden (not to be confused with the other definition of midden, which is an area of animal droppings).

Red squirrels usually nest in hollow or fallen trees, but they also make leaf nests similar to those of gray squirrels. In the extreme northern part of their range they will make a nest under their midden so that their stored food is readily available to them without having to leave their nest. They are not hunted as heavily as gray squirrels and fox squirrels. Their normal diet of pine cones and pine seeds can impart a flavor to their meat that some find unappetizing or unpalatable.

•••

About *squirrel* hunting

Today's squirrel hunters may not think much about it, but they are continuing a long and noble tradition with its roots in the exploration and settlement of North America.

For the early settlers and frontiersmen, it was often the humble and ubiquitous squirrel — more so than deer or elk, more than buffalo or bear or wild turkey — that ensured their survival and the survival of their families as they pushed west into the wilderness of the eastern mountains and beyond. When big game was scarce, these early woodsmen could almost always fill their trenchers with fresh squirrel meat. Out of necessity, they learned to be successful squirrel hunters.

Their woods craft and marksmanship were vital to the settlement of the continent, and even played a pivotal role in the fight for independence and the founding of the United States of America. The militiamen — the 'Overmountain Boys' and other citizen soldiers — who defeated the British army at such battles as Kings Mountain and Cowpens were seasoned woodsmen who first acquired their sharpshooting skills by putting squirrel on the table.

Squirrel hunting hasn't really changed much since the times of the hunter pioneers. We have different weapons now, of course; most of us don't use a large bore muzzleloader to *bark* squirrels* out of a tree. But basic squirrel hunting strategy is still the same, and it's pretty simple: Find 'em and shoot 'em. How you accomplish this, however, depends on your tactics.

There are three basic methods for hunting squirrels: Still hunting, stand hunting, and dog hunting.

Many squirrel hunters like to stalk their quarry. They move quietly through the woods and usually cover a lot of ground looking for feeding activity, and take their shots as they encounter squirrels. This is called still hunting. Others prefer to stand hunt, which is a less strenuous and often more productive approach. They find an area with a concentration of nests and dens or an abundance of feeding sign, then settle down and wait patiently for squirrels to show themselves. The third method, dog hunting, incorporates some elements of both still hunting and stand hunting. Except, in this style of hunting a good squirrel dog does the stalking; it finds the squirrels and chases them to a tree. The hunter

---

* The frontiersmen and mountaineers usually owned only one gun that they could use to put meat on the table, and it normally was a large caliber weapon that was powerful enough for big game like deer and bear. But these hunters knew that putting a large caliber ball into a small squirrel would destroy a lot of meat, and meat, after all, was their goal. So they often used a technique called 'barking' to bag squirrels. They simply shot at a spot very near the squirrel so that the bark or wood exploding from the impact of the ball knocked the squirrel to the ground where it then could be finished off. And, being naturally frugal—shot and powder was valuable and not to be wasted—they picked their shots carefully; they only barked squirrels that were on a log or a tree trunk or branch near the ground, so that the lead ball could be recovered easily and later recast and reused. A shotgun hunter today can use this technique with good effect for close range shots.

simply waits until the dog barks "treed," then hurries to the spot and stand hunts, waiting for the squirrel to present a target. Dog hunting can be used anytime but often works best late in the season when the trees are bare and squirrels spend a lot of time foraging on the ground.

Squirrel hunting combines all of the skills needed to be a success in the pursuit of bigger, more elusive game — stealth, the ability to read animal sign, accuracy with a firearm, knowledge of animal habits and habitat, patience, self-reliance....

Squirrel hunting is still one of the best ways to become an experienced woodsman, marksman, and all-around hunter.

•••

Tips

1 — Scout your hunting areas before the season opens.

Squirrels inhabit areas where food and shelter are readily available. Scout the woods during the pre-season and look for the mast trees that squirrels depend on for food and nesting sites.

Bear in mind, what may have been a productive hunting ground last season may be virtually barren this year.

Squirrels sometimes abandon nests and dens that they have used for years if they foster disease or become flea-infested. And sometimes squirrels are evicted from their nests or dens by other animals, such as woodpeckers, owls and raccoons. Search for mast trees containing dreys that appear well tended and in good repair and dens that show signs of recent or current use: the entrance holes are smooth and un-weathered, or raw wood is visible where squirrels have gnawed away bark to enlarge the entrance, or bits of shed fur are caught on the bark near the opening where squirrels have passed in and out.

Also, be aware that there are good years when nuts and fruits are plentiful, and bad years when drought, wildfires, insect infestation, diseases or other factors, such as the cyclical nature of mast crop production, make abundant squirrel forage hard to find. A good acorn crop, for example, generally occurs about every four years, an abundant beechnut crop about every seven years.

In an abundant year, when there is more than enough food to go around, squirrels will be widespread and relatively inactive. They won't have to travel far for food, and they won't have to compete with each other for food. But when food is scarce, the squirrel population will be concentrated where the food source is located, and the squirrels will contend aggressively with each other for every available morsel. In other words, squirrels will be less active when a lot of food is right at their doorstep, so to speak, and other squirrels aren't crowding them, and more active when there are several other squirrels in the area and mast is limited.

Find the food sources and the active nests before the season opens; the squirrels will be there when it's time to start hunting them.

2 — ALWAYS be on the lookout for poisonous snakes.

A snake bite can bring a beautiful day in the woods to a painful and possibly fatal end.

During pre-season scouting, or while hunting early in the season before the first hard frosts, poisonous snakes may still be active. Watch where you step! Get in the habit of stepping *onto* a log or rock, not *over* it, and look down before you step off. Believe me, a stepped-on snake gets really irritated, really fast!

[Once, many years ago, when I was but a lad, one of my hunting buddies stepped on a copperhead snake while we were climbing the wooded hillside behind my house. Luckily, he just happened to step on the snake's head; otherwise, I'm sure he would have been nipped

before we even knew the snake was there—a copperhead's camouflage makes it almost invisible against the brown, dead leaves.

He was ahead of me and we were climbing a fairly steep slope, so I was almost eye-level with the snake when it began to twist and writhe under his foot. I told him to stop, not to move, and he instantly froze and looked down. The snake—a good 3-footer if it was an inch—was thrashing its body around his shoe, trying to pull free and get away (or bite something, more likely). Stepping down harder, he kept the snake pinned against the ground long enough for me to separate the body from the head with my pocketknife. We couldn't think of any other way to get away from the snake without risking a bite.

Can't remember how many squirrels we shot that day, or if we got any at all. The snake encounter was the highlight of that hunt.]

Even late in the year, if the days have been unseasonably warm, you might encounter a copperhead, a rattlesnake or, if you're close to a slow-moving stream, lake or pond, a cottonmouth water moccasin. This is especially true if you hunt in the Deep South where fall and winter are normally mild and where, of course, you also need to be watchful for coral snakes.

The copperhead inhabits woody and rocky areas in the Eastern Gulf States, Texas, Arkansas, Maryland, north Florida, Illinois, Indiana, Oklahoma, Kansas, Ohio, Kentucky, New York, Alabama, Tennessee, and Massachusetts. It is predominately brown in color with deeper, richer brown bands that are narrow on top and wider at the bottom. The top of the head is a coppery color, hence the name. Averaging about 30 inches in length, the copperhead is usually fairly docile but will defend itself if threatened. Its venom is hemotoxic, which means that the venom destroys red blood cells and produces serious tissue damage, which is prone to gangrene. Few people actually die from the bite of a copperhead; however, the bite is painful and the venom will make you desperately ill. And if you're especially sensitive to the venom—for example, if you have severe allergic reactions to bee stings—a snake bite could be fatal unless you get medical help quickly.

The cottonmouth water moccasin is a semi-aquatic cousin of the copperhead. Adult snakes are uniformly olive brown or almost black. Young water moccasins are strongly cross-banded with dark brown. It can be found in or near swamps, lakes, rivers and ditches in southeast Virginia, west central Alabama, south Georgia, Illinois, east central Kentucky, Ohio, south central Oklahoma, Texas, North and South Carolina, Florida, and the Florida Keys. It averages about three feet in length, up to a maximum of about six feet. Its venom is hemotoxic and more powerful than a copperhead's. The cottonmouth gets its name from its habit, when threatened or aroused, of drawing its head close to its body and opening its mouth wide to show the white interior.

Many different species of rattlesnakes are found throughout North America. They are all poisonous. In most states where squirrels are hunted, the timber rattlesnake, the eastern diamondback, the western diamondback, and the Massasauga rattlesnake are the species most frequently encountered. Depending on the species, rattlesnakes can be from two feet to seven feet in length. For all species, color is generally darkish brown or almost black. Rattlesnake venom is a potent hemotoxin and, generally, the larger the rattler, the more venom it will inject when it bites. A bite from a rattlesnake is extremely painful and produces considerable tissue damage. Don't depend on a rattlesnake to warn you of its presence; they don't always rattle before striking.

[Another hunting partner almost found out the hard way about this 'exception to the rule.'

It was early in the season and we were hunting the woods along an old fire road that ran through the state forest. When we reached what appeared to be good squirrel habitat, we split up. He moved into the woods on one side of the road, while I worked the woods on the other side.

We hadn't been separated more than a quarter of on hour when I heard the distinctive boom of his trusty old .410 single shot. "Got one!" I thought. I had a lot of confidence in his skill and proficiency with that small bore scattergun. I hunted a while longer, but, not having much luck, I worked my way back to the road and began searching for a more productive area. A couple minutes later I heard the rustle of dry leaves a short distance behind me and turned to see my partner emerge from the woods carrying, not a fat fox squirrel as I had expected, but a rather long, thick bodied rattler, sans head.

He had spotted some squirrel activity but didn't have a dear shot, he explained a couple of minutes later as he stretched out the bloody, headless reptile in front of me on the dusty road. When he started to move closer, he said, a small movement on the ground in front of him caused him to look down. And there, directly beneath his poised right foot, was a coiled rattler. The movement that had alerted him was the snake drawing back its head slightly to strike. He said he stepped back slowly, cocking the shotgun's hammer and bringing the muzzle down at the same time...and fired.

At no time, he complained, had the rattlesnake 'rattled' to warn him away.]

The coral snake is widespread in southeast North Carolina, the Gulf States, west central Mississippi,

Florida, the Florida Keys, and Texas. It can be identified by its vivid markings of black, yellow and red bands. It is normally very shy and secretive and seldom seen, so many people who believe they have seen a coral snake have actually encountered one of its non-poisonous look-a-likes — a scarlet snake or a scarlet king snake. The colors are the same but the patterns are not, and it's hard to discern the difference in a quick, often panicked glance. The first color on a coral snake, starting at the nose, is black. Narrow yellow bands separate the red and black bands. The first and last color on both the scarlet snake and the scarlet king snake is red (red nose and red tail tip), and the red bands never touch the yellow bands (the red and yellow are separated by black). The colored bands on both the coral snake and the scarlet king snake go all the way around the body; the scarlet snake has a white underside. To know whether you need to worry if you encounter a brightly banded red, black and yellow snake, just remember the warning: "Red on yellow, kill a fellow; red on black, venom lack."

All snakes are beneficial and even the poisonous ones should not be harmed. Unless you're in imminent danger of being bitten. The best advice if you encounter a snake, any kind of snake, while hunting is: Leave it alone. Don't threaten it. Walk around and away from the snake, giving it a wide berth. And don't try to catch it!

3 — ALWAYS carry a first aid kit.

Accidents can happen, especially in the woods while hunting. A fallen branch or loose stone can twist your ankle; a fall can break your leg or arm. You can cut yourself while skinning a squirrel; you can accidentally shoot yourself (or a careless hunter can shoot you); you can become seriously ill....

If you're on your own, if no one is there to render aid or transport you to a hospital, if there's no way to 'call 911,' what do you do?

Without a first aid kit, not much.

But if you had the foresight to tuck a small first aid kit in your hunting pack, you'd be able to wrap a sprained ankle, maybe splint and immobilize a broken bone, apply a patch of moleskin to a painful blister, put a bandage on a bleeding gash, treat a nagging headache...well, you get the idea.

A well-equipped first aid kit need not be large or bulky; in fact, you'll be more inclined to carry one if it is lightweight and compact enough to slip into a belt pack or a pocket of your hunting jacket.

You can buy a ready-made first aid kit; there are a lot of them available. You can find them at any pharmacy or at Wal-Mart, and the American Red Cross has some pricey ones for sale. But most ready-made kits seem overpriced, and either too large with too much extra 'stuff' to carry comfortably or too small to contain the variety and quantity of supplies you may actually need, or they simply include a mish-mash of bandages and gauze pads and ointments of dubious quality and utility — more *show* than *go*, so to speak.

But, if you give a little thought to your emergency medical needs, the types of medical emergencies that might befall you while out in the woods, your first aid skill level and your financial resources, then purchase your supplies accordingly, you can put together a first-rate first aid kit that incorporates the virtues of portability, quality and utility

Here's a model that would serve as a starting point for a basic hunter's first aid kit:

1 - 3-inch elastic bandage

Adhesive bandages, assorted sizes

Sterilized gauze pads

2 - 1-, 2-, 3-inch gauze roll bandages

Butterfly laceration dressings

Sterilized dressings, several sizes

Safety pins

Small folding scissors

Tweezers

Cleansing agent

1 small bottle of topical antiseptic

1 eye dressing

Moleskin (for blisters)

1 triangular bandage

Chewable antacid tablets

Aspirin, acetaminophen, or ibuprofen

A pocket-size first aid manual

You can customize this kit as needed. For example, include any prescription medication you might need while away from home, such as allergy or high blood pressure medicine. If you're hunting early in the season when mosquitoes, gnats, chiggers, ticks and fleas can be a nuisance, add a powerful insect repellant to your kit.

Replace first aid supplies as they're used so that the kit is always complete when you're ready to hunt.

Finally, as important as it is to have a first aid kit with you in case of a medical emergency, it is virtually useless unless you have a practical understanding of how to use it. Take the time to learn some basic first aid.

A first aid kit is a necessary piece of hunting gear. Don't go hunting — don't even go into the woods — without one.

4 — In late summer and early fall, add a snake-bite kit to your first aid kit.

Most medical experts agree that using a snakebite kit is a last resort measure only. The best advice for a snakebite victim, according the American Red Cross, is:

1) Wash the bite with soap and water

2) Immobilize the bitten area and keep it lower than the heart, and

3) Get medical help.

But if it's impossible to reach a hospital quickly, the American Red Cross recommends two other measures:

If the snake bite victim is unable to get medical help within 30 minutes, a bandage should be wrapped two to four inches above the bite to slow the spread of the venom. The bandage should not be so tight that it cuts off blood flow; it should be loose enough to allow you to slip a finger under it.

A suction device like the ones found in commercial

snakebite kits can be used to help draw the venom out of the wound.

These commercial snakebite kits also usually include a small blade for cutting and opening the wound; however, in recent years medical professionals have begun to discount the value of this kind of invasive treatment because it can be more harmful to the victim than the snakebite alone.

And forget about sucking out the poison orally. Some of the venom could be absorbed through a sore on or in the mouth or ingested by involuntarily swallowing it.

5 — Don't forget water when you go hunting.

Even if the weather is cool, after a few hours and a few miles trudging uphill and downhill, you're going to get thirsty.

Carry a canteen filled with tap water or put a couple of plastic bottles of store-bought water in your hunting pack. If you don't have some drinking water with you, you may be tempted to slake your thirst from any little creek or spring you come across while hunting. Not a good idea! The water may look clean, bubbling and splashing over the stones. It may look clean and clear and pure—but is it?

Probably not!

Untreated water is often host to some particularly pernicious parasites, bacteria and viruses, against which we have little natural defense. Giardia, a tiny parasite, is one. Can you say *diarrhea*? How about *dysentery*?

Other water-borne diseases are cholera, typhoid, shigella, polio, meningitis, and hepatitis A and E.

A lot of streams and other natural water sources, even those in seemingly remote areas, may be contaminated with human or animal excrement or even industrial chemicals. This is especially true of streams or springs near agricultural areas where herbicides and pesticides can run off or leach into the groundwater.

Don't take a chance on untested water. Carry potable water with you.

Or, if you don't like the idea of lugging around an additional two or three pounds of weight (water weighs about eight pounds per gallon), consider buying and using a small water filter/purifier. A number of models have been developed for use in survival kits or for backpackers and other outdoorsmen who like to travel light.

Most of these water filter/purifiers use activated charcoal to remove silt, some chemicals and many dangerous organisms from the water. The charcoal also improves the taste of the water. They will not, however, filter out all types of bacteria and are much too porous to eliminate any viruses.

One popular model looks something like a soda straw and is used the same way. You simply insert one end of the 'straw' into the water and draw the water up through the filter element into your mouth. It's lightweight and compact and would be a good choice for a hunter.

But regardless of the type of water filter/purifier you decide on, choose your water source carefully. Always avoid standing water—a lake or a pond...or a mud puddle. Drink from freely running water only

6 — Get your body in shape.

Squirrel hunting usually involves a lot of strenuous walking and climbing. Get in shape before the season starts.

Pre-season scouting excursions can help you with physical conditioning. Walk the forest and fields, climb the hills, ford the creeks, and find the locations that will be hotspots when the season opens. And carry with you what you would normally carry when hunting: your hunting pack, your jacket (you don't have to wear it, just carry it, maybe strapped to your pack), your gun and ammunition, water, first aid kit, etc. If you normally wear hunting boots when you hunt, wear them when you scout. Get your body used to the extra weight.

If you can't get out into the woods often enough during the pre-season to get into condition for hunting, use any stairs in your home as an exercise aid to build up your legs and your wind. If you exercise in this way, again, remember to carry your gun (unloaded), or something of similar weight and heft, and other gear you normally carry with while hunting.

Twenty pounds of additional weight from your gun, ammunition, water, hunting pack and even hunting boots can take its toll on your body if you're not used to carrying it.

7 — Get your eyes in shape.

Hunting, especially squirrel hunting, requires good eyesight.

Get your eyes checked well in advance of hunting season so that if your prescription has changed since the last check-up, you will be able to get accustomed to new eyeglasses or contact lenses for target practice and for hunting.

If you need glasses, by all means wear them while hunting.

8 — Wear shooting glasses.

The gun range is not the only place you need shooting, or safety, glasses. You need eye protection while you're hunting, too. Most shooting glasses are available with clear lenses or amber (yellow) lenses. For squirrel hunting, the amber tint is a good choice. It improves contrast in the low-light conditions you will encounter under a heavy leaf canopy early in the season and in flat-light conditions caused by fog or misty rain.

9 — Look for squirrel sign.

When scouting for squirrels, look for 'cut' nuts and any active nests or dens that may be in the area.

Squirrels like nuts, all kinds of nuts—hickory nuts, walnuts, beechnuts, acorns—which they not only eat daily but also store for the winter. An abundance of nut hull fragments, or cut nuts, around nut-producing trees in the late summer when the nuts start to ripen indicates squirrel feeding activity and, therefore, a good area to concentrate your hunting when the season begins.

Also, learn to recognize active dreys or dens in the area. There will be considerable activity to and from the nests during the season as the squirrels that inhabit them bury or retrieve nuts from their nearby caches.

10 — Know the law.

Before the season begins, study the hunting laws. They change slightly almost every year, and, as law enforcement officers are fond of pointing out, "ignorance of the law is no excuse..."

It's your responsibility to stay up-to-date on your state's hunting rules and regulations. Know the current bag limits for the areas you plan to hunt—a reduced squirrel population may necessitate reducing from the previous year the number of squirrels you can legally harvest. Know which types of firearms are legal to use—an increase in the *human* population near the areas you normally hunt may cause the state to restrict the area to 'shotgun only,' where the year before you were allowed to take squirrels with a rifle or pistol, or prohibit hunting in that area entirely

Have any changes been made affecting the use of handguns? Are there any special seasons or restrictions for unconventional hunting weapons like long bows, crossbows, air rifles, or muzzleloaders?

Always get a current copy of hunting regulations and review it before you start hunting. The regulations are available from your state's wildlife resources or fish-and-game offices, on the Internet, at sporting goods stores, or at discount stores that sell sporting goods, such as Wal-Mart. And, they're free.

11 — Practice, practice, practice.

Use the off-season months to hone your shooting skills.

Go to a shooting range regularly, sight in your .22 or pattern your shotgun, and do some serious target practice. Work on breath control, and practice shooting from different positions—standing, sitting, kneeling, and prone. Practice on moving targets and stationary targets; practice shooting offhand and with support. The more you shoot, the better you will know your hunting weapon and the more accurate you will be.

If you don't yet practice the 'one shot, one kill' philosophy of your hunting forebears, work at it. Always try to make your first shot count. It's more economical and more productive. And, it's definitely safer for everyone sharing the woods with you. 'Spray-and-pray' shooting is for amateurs.

Practice is the only way to acquire the confidence and skill you need to consistently make your first shot a killing shot, or at least a hit.

12 — Plan each shot.

In other words, before you squeeze off a round, you should know where and what that bullet or load of shot is going to hit, if you miss your target.

Every hunter misses the target sometimes. So plan for it. Know where nearby farms or houses or public roads are located and their distance relative to your hunting area and avoid shooting toward them. Always try to maneuver into a shooting position that gives you a backstop for your shot—a tree trunk or thick branch, a hillside.

A .22 caliber bullet can travel up to a mile. Shotgun pellets will come to earth in a much shorter distance, but that's no consolation to a nearby hunter (or an innocent bystander) who gets 'rained on' by a shower of pellets at the end of their trajectory. Even falling shot or a spent bullet is dangerous.

13 — Identify your target.

Shoot only at what you can actually see and identify as your quarry. This is good advice no matter what kind of hunting you're doing.

Shooting into a nest or a clump of leaves in which a squirrel is hiding, or may be hiding, with the hope of making a lucky shot or scaring a squirrel into the open, is NOT a good idea—you might even actually kill a squirrel in a nest but have no way to recover it—and neither is shooting at a lump or a bump on a tree trunk or branch, because you *think* it might be a squirrel.

This kind of hunting behavior is irresponsible and unsportsmanlike. It's dangerous. And, again, it's what amateurs do.

14 — Use binoculars to locate and identify squirrels.

Binoculars can be a big help when scouting for squirrels.

With a good set of binoculars you can scan the surrounding forest for a considerable distance to locate feeding squirrels or active nests and dens, without moving around and making noise.

You don't need large, powerful binoculars for this job. Some of the small, lightweight, fold-up-style binoculars would serve well; so would a small monocular scope, for that matter. Both are reasonably priced, even cheap, and the quality of the optics is more than adequate.

15 — Carry a knife (or two).

The most useful tool a squirrel hunter can have — other than a rifle, shotgun or other weapon for actually harvesting squirrels — is a knife. In fact, I can't imagine that any serious hunter or outdoorsman would willingly go into the woods or fields without one.

A knife is a necessity if you spend any time in the outdoors, but carrying a couple of different kinds of knives, if they're the right kinds, definitely has its advantages when you hunt.

While I am usually a big fan of big blades, experience and common sense have shown that a large hunting/skinning knife with a 6- to 9-inch blade, which may be ideal for field dressing a deer or butchering a feral hog, is a less-than-ideal choice for use on small game like squirrels. A large knife is just too cumbersome and awkward to use for this kind of job.

Instead, carry a belt knife with a 3- or 4-inch fixed or folding-blade as your primary squirrel hunting knife. It's small enough to do some deft skinning work but still has the heft to cut easily through the flesh and small bones of a tough bushy tail. And this size knife still can be used for other heavy-duty cutting chores while in the woods, such as cutting and trimming a small sapling for use as a walking stick or a makeshift rifle monopod,

A drop point-style blade is best: If you use a knife with an upswept blade tip to field dress a squirrel, it's easy, way too easy, to inadvertently nick the squirrel's innards and allow the contents to taint the meat. *Yuck!*

If you carry a folding-blade hunting knife, just make sure it is lockable, so the blade can't close on your fingers while you're using it.

The second knife you should have with you while squirrel hunting is a small pocketknife, preferably one with multiple blades. Use it for light-duty cutting chores, such as removing the musk glands from a squirrel carcass, digging out a painful splinter, or augmenting your first aid kit (keep one of the blades *scalpel-sharp*).

One of the Swiss Army-style knives or a good quality 'multi-tool' is also a good choice for your second knife, because it offers a selection of other handy, useful tools, such as tweezers, screwdrivers, and an awl or punch, in addition to one or two knife blades.

But no matter what type of knife or knives you carry with you while hunting, it's important that the knife is *sharp*. A sharp knife can do more work, and do it more effortlessly and more efficiently, than a dull one.

And a sharp knife is much, much safer to use than a dull knife.

That sounds contradictory, doesn't it?

But, it's true.

A knife with a keen edge requires less force to do its cutting job and, therefore, is easier to control. A dull knife, on the other hand, requires that you apply more force to compensate for its lack of sharpness, and the more muscle you have to put behind the knife the less control you have over the blade. Even a dull knife can still easily slice or puncture *your* flesh, if it has enough out-of-control force behind it.

So add a small whetstone to your hunting equipment. Then, if your knife starts to dull during use, whip out that stone, give the blade a few swipes to restore the edge, and continue cutting...safely.

16 — Always watch for movement...

The human eye can detect movement from a considerable distance.

A motionless squirrel is practically invisible on a branch or against the trunk of a tree; squirrel camouflage is that good. But even a slight movement will draw the eye to it and cause the squirrel to seemingly 'materialize' out of the confusing backdrop of leaves and interlaced branches.

And, oddly, it's easier to detect movement from the edge of the eye than by looking straight on. So keep your eyes moving back and forth continually as you search the branches ahead, above or below you for activity. When you catch movement with the 'tail of your eye,' focus on the location and take your shot when the squirrel presents itself.

Even if you are still hunting, you should watch more than you walk. In late summer and early autumn, locate squirrels by looking for moving branches and shaking leaves. Even a small squirrel can create a lot of movement when it jumps from one branch or one tree to another.

17 — ...and listen!

You don't have to see squirrels first to find them. Often, sound will give away a squirrel's presence. The noises of squirrels barking or busily cutting nuts or moving through the trees can be heard from a long distance away, and in early autumn before the trees have shed their foliage you often can locate your quarry simply by listening for them. Listen for the *snap-slap* of nut hulls and whole nuts falling through the leafy canopy or the rustle of leaves as a squirrel bounds from one branch to another or their distinctive barks.

As you move through the woods, stop often and simply listen. When you hear the rustle of shaking leaves or the distinctive sound of nut cutting, like heavy raindrops or hailstones falling through the leaves, or barking, move toward the sound quietly until you see the squirrel that's causing the noise, and then maneuver (again, as quietly as possible) until you get a clear shot.

Especially when still hunting, a good technique is to take a step or two, then remain motionless for the time it would take to move three or four steps, and listen for squirrel sound. Use this pause to re-orient yourself, confirm the direction to the sound and estimate the distance.

If the sound of nut cutting suddenly stops while you are making your approach, it may mean the squirrel has detected your movement and is alarmed and wary. Stop moving when the cutting sounds stop and remain motionless. Continue your approach when the cutting resumes and can help cover any noise you make.

18 — Hunt from a higher vantage point.

Whenever you can, take advantage of hillsides and ridgelines and high stream banks.

Even early in the season while leaves are still on the trees, a higher vantage point allows you to see farther. And, by looking *down* into the treetops you can often spot movement that would be hard to see otherwise.

19 — In late fall and early winter watch the ground for squirrels.

When the trees are bare, squirrels spend a lot of time on the forest floor looking for food. They will search for acorns and nuts that they cached earlier in the season. They will look for nuts that fell from the trees when ripe and lie exposed on the dead leaves. And sometimes they'll look for edible fungi.

Although you may sight squirrels in the trees going to or from their dens, they will be searching on the ground a lot longer than they will be traveling in the trees, so direct your attention downward. Watch for movement and listen for the start-and-stop sounds of a squirrel hopping through the dry leaves or digging for its cached nuts.

20 — For springtime hunting action, find the den trees first.

Squirrels forage differently in the spring than they do in the fall.

Nuts and acorns from the previous year are still available, but they are now on the ground, scattered and scarce. Consequently, squirrels will be searching for food on the forest floor. And since the nuts and acorns are scattered hither and yon, the squirrels searching for them will be widely dispersed, too. In other words, squirrels are going to be 'few and far between,' and you will probably have to spend a lot of time looking for them.

But if you can locate a concentration of den trees before the season opens, that's where you will find a lot of squirrels when the spring season begins.

20 — In the spring, look for active dens while you hunt.

If you don't have the time or the opportunity to locate active den trees before the spring season arrives, you can find them while you hunt.

Forget about stand hunting—you could wait a long time before a squirrel just happens by. And still hunting can waste a lot of time, too. Instead, look around for stands of mature mast trees, the potential den trees, and get to them quickly. Look for squirrel activity there. If there are no dens in the trees, or if you locate dens that appear to have been abandoned, move on.

Find trees with active dens and you will find where squirrels are resting and feeding.

22 — Still hunt on damp days when your movement creates little noise.

A good soaking rainfall during the night can make your morning hunt more productive.

Stealth is an essential part of successful squirrel hunting, and walking on sodden dead leaves is quieter than walking on leaves that are dry and crackly. Dead leaves that are wet from even a light rain will stay wet – and quiet – longer than dead leaves that are merely dew-damp. Consequently, you can still hunt more quietly for a longer period of time.

On dry days, get to your hunting area early. Get out in the woods before the fog burns away and the dew dries off the dead leaves. If you've already picked out a tree or patch of trees with good squirrel sign where you plan to focus your hunt, get to it early while the leaves are still damp and quiet. Then sit tight and let the unsuspecting squirrels come to you.

24 — For greater success, hunt when squirrels are most active.

Early morning and late afternoon are usually the best times to hunt squirrels, because that's when squirrels are the most active.

Red and gray squirrel activity generally peaks two hours after sunrise and two to five hours before sunset. Fox squirrels are normally fairly active throughout the day, but, still, their activity peaks about mid-morning.

25 — Weather can help, or hinder, your hunt.

Rainy, stormy days are usually poor squirrel hunting days. Most squirrels, unless they are desperate for food, will stick close to the den or nest. They don't like to be out in nasty, wet weather any more than we do.

The time following a light rain, however, is normally excellent for squirrel hunting. The dead leaves underfoot are wet and quiet, allowing you to move about almost silently, and the squirrels start moving around again in their never-ending quest for food. Drops of water falling through the leaves can make it difficult, however, to locate squirrel activity by sound alone.

An early snow can help your hunt. You can move a lot more quietly over a light blanket of fresh snow than you can over bare dead dry leaves. And an early snow won't diminish squirrel activity, since food is still available.

A windy day normally is not a good hunting day. It's hard to tell whether movement in the branches is caused by the wind or by a squirrel. And squirrels tend to stay closer to the den or nest when the wind is strong and gusting.

26 — Talk to local farmers and other hunters.

If you are going to be hunting in an area that you've never hunted before, talk to the folks that live around there. Ask the locals about squirrel populations and activity, nearby private or restricted property, etc. Often they can pinpoint a hotspot for you, saving many hours of fruitless hunting.

27 — Private property offers some of the best hunting.

Although hunting in game preserves and other wildlife management areas can be good, hunting on private property is often the best.

The hunting pressure on squirrel populations on private property normally is much less than on public hunting lands; therefore, the squirrels are often more plentiful and less skittish, affording you greater opportunities for good shots and a big harvest with less effort.

28 — Respect private property.

Trespassing is a serious offense! ALWAYS get permission before hunting on private property!

And, if you want to be a good neighbor, if you want to be welcomed back, don't leave behind any trash (in fact, it's a good idea to pack out any trash you find), don't start any fires, don't damage any fences, and DONT, EVER, shoot towards the property owner's residence, outbuildings or livestock.

29 — Simple courtesy is never a waste of time.

If a landowner allows you to hunt on his property, repay that kindness with an offer to share your harvest with him.

Many country folk might not have time to hunt themselves, but would appreciate the makings of a squirrel fricassee in recognition of and recompense for their generosity. It's just simple courtesy and excellent public relations. And a gift of food, even in these days and times, is a true gift.

30 — Don't crowd other hunters.

If you walk up on another hunter — even if he has staked out the hunting spot *you* had planned to hunt — don't crowd him. Greet him silently and move on quietly.

Remember the Golden Rule: "Do unto others as you would have them do unto you."

You can always check the area later if the hunter has left. Or, just make sure you get to *your* hotspot earlier the next time.

31 — Let someone know your whereabouts.

Always let a family member or friend know where you plan to hunt and when you expect to be back.

Accidents can happen; if you suffer a mishap while hunting, someone needs to know when to start worrying and where to start searching for you.

32 — Rushed shots mean lost and crippled squirrels.

Any kind of hunting is an exercise in patience; and patience is definitely a virtue when it comes to squirrel hunting.

If you locate a squirrel that is hidden from you, concealed in leaves in the upper branches of a tree, relax, be patient. You'll usually get a clear shot if you wait long enough.

And when the squirrel does finally present you with a target, don't rush your shot. Take your time and aim! Unless you are a very skilled 'snap shooter' (and most of us are not), a hurried shot will usually result in a complete miss or, worse, a wounded squirrel. Make your shot with cool, calm deliberation, not desperation.

33 — Concentrate your hunt where there is a squirrel highway.

That's right—a squirrel highway!

Squirrels seem to love fences—rail fences, picket fences, even barbed wire fences. In squirrel territory, a fence of any kind becomes a bushy tail expressway, an easy, obstacle-free route that they use regularly to move from one area in their territory to another in the never-ending search for food, water or places to cache nuts for the winter.

If any fences run through your hunting area, concentrate your hunt there. After all, a squirrel perched on a fence post presents a more open target than one high in the branches overhead.

34 — Find the other travel routes squirrels use.

Squirrels use other travel routes in addition to fences. Find these 'travel corridors' in your hunting area and you'll be rewarded with a fairly steady procession of squirrels moving between different areas in their home range. Typical travel corridors include wood lines that separate cornfields, windrows on the edges of fields, or brushy streambeds and drainage ditches bordering agricultural land.

35 — Don't ignore other forage when looking for squirrel hotspots.

Squirrels eat more than just nuts and acorns, although these are primary food sources.

Squirrels also feed on tree blossoms and buds (in the spring), berries (throughout the summer and fall), fruits and field corn (in late summer and early fall), various vegetable and flower seeds (such as sunflowers, *yum!*) and fungi.

Keep other food sources in mind when scouting and selecting a hunting area.

36 — Look for a nearby fresh water source.

Squirrels, like any other animal, need water.

Gray squirrels and red squirrels are seldom far from it. Groves of mast trees, such as oaks and hickories, growing along a creek, river, lake or pond are good areas to look for gray squirrels.

Fox squirrels range more widely so a nearby water source is not as crucial for them.

37 — Fox squirrels are especially fond of corn.

A prime habitat for fox squirrels is wood lines that border cornfields; midmornings are usually best, although fox squirrels are generally somewhat active throughout the day.

Even after a corn crop is harvested, there are spills of kernels and, often, whole ears of corn left behind. Consequently, you'll find fox squirrels on the ground, sometimes hundreds of yards from the safety of the trees, taking advantage of this 'windfall' — a tasty, very accessible smorgasbord of sweet crunchy 'niblets.'

38 — Learn as much as you can about squirrel habitat.

The more you know about squirrel habitat the more successful hunter you'll be.

Remember, gray squirrels generally prefer dense, mature forests with a lot of undergrowth — brush, briars, small saplings and the like.

Fox squirrels normally can be found in more open woodlands and in areas where there is a mix of forest and agricultural land. In some areas where fox squirrels do inhabit dense forest, they seem to prefer the ridges, leaving the valleys to the grays.

Red squirrels are also called pine squirrels for a reason — they inhabit pine and mixed coniferous and deciduous forests and feed primarily on seeds and pinecones.

39 — Squirrel activity depends a lot on weather conditions.

In bad weather — rain, sleet, heavy snow, strong gusting winds — the gray squirrel will den up and not move about much until the weather clears. Fox squirrels are active at all times of the year, in even the bitterest of weather.

40 — Take notes.

Carry a small notebook and pen or pencil so you can make notes about where squirrels are killed or seen.

Jot down the locations of squirrel sign, the weather, the time, landmarks you use to find your productive hunting areas, etc.

The notes will be helpful when preparing for future hunts.

41 — Change your hunting style to match the conditions.

The availability of food and the corresponding level of squirrel activity may force a change in the way you hunt. Be prepared to switch tactics.

If you normally still hunt, i.e., stalk squirrels by moving as quietly as possible through the woods and cover a lot of ground, squirrel inactivity may mean that you have to stand hunt—find a tree in which maybe one or more squirrels are leisurely cutting nuts, and wait for your shots.

If stand hunting is your preference and forage is sparse, squirrels will be moving around a lot, trying to get their share of the available food and competing with each other for every precious nut or acorn. In this case, you'll have a number of energetic, nervous, scampering targets moving from tree to tree, which means you need to move, too, if you want to bag your limit.

42 — Look for more than one squirrel.

Often there will be more than one squirrel in the same tree or a nearby tree. It's often productive when sighting on one squirrel to fix the location of a second one for a quick follow-up shot.

In what some hunters call a 'honey tree,' one that's laden with nuts and host to a number of squirrels cutting and feeding together, you may be able to get most of your limit without moving more than a few paces, if you're patient and willing to wait and mark where your shot squirrels fall.

43 — Still hunt early when other game is moving around.

The noise of moving game is a familiar one to other animals, and that can help the hunter, whose movements can resemble that of large game, to get closer before the squirrels become alarmed and scamper for cover.

If you hunt during times that other game animals are active — usually early morning and late in the afternoon, you stand a better chance of sneaking up on squirrels.

44 — Imitate the movements of other animals.

When we walk, we humans tend to march, trudge, shuffle along at a relatively steady pace. We're used to getting from Point A to Point B as effortlessly and quickly as possible. You need to break this habit when you're in the woods hunting. The other animals that share the forest with squirrels don't walk that way — *ain't natural!* A steady *clomp-crunch, clomp-crunch* of a big clumsy human striding through the dry leaves is a tip-off to every squirrel in earshot that danger is nearby. And they're going to become very wary and hide until they sense that danger is past. Deer, rabbits, birds, squirrels, and other woodland animals — when they're moving, they are generally foraging unhurriedly for food. They tend to move in starts and stops. Try to imitate the way they sound when they move through the forest and you'll surprise more squirrels.

45 — Don't overlook midday hunting.

If the only time you have available for hunting is in the middle part of the day, don't fret.

Although squirrels are normally more active early in the morning and late in the afternoon and evening, there is almost always some activity, such as nut cutting or searching for caches, during the midday hours. This is especially true of fox squirrels.

You may just have to hunt harder, and smarter, during the midday hours.

46 — To boost activity, try calling squirrels.

When the action is slow and squirrels remain hidden, you may be able to locate them by using a squirrel call.

Some experienced squirrel hunters use a store-bought call that is supposed to sound like a young squirrel that is hurt or in trouble, which, it is claimed, will arouse and anger older squirrels. At least, that's the theory.

Some hunters can imitate the bark of a squirrel by striking the edges of two 50-cent pieces or two pebbles together. Some hunters claim that making a squeaking or chirping sound by 'kissing' your hand between the thumb and forefinger will sometimes cause squirrels to bark and give away their location.

Worth a try if the squirrels are shy and reluctant to show

themselves.

[I've never mastered any of these techniques myself, but my dad could make a squeaky, Donald Duck sort of barking sound that often got a response from squirrels hidden in the treetops.]

47 — Avoid smoking while hunting.

Although squirrels depend primarily on their sight to identify danger, they also have a keen sense of smell. The smell of smoke in the air is a danger signal for all woodland animals, including squirrels.

And, as Smokey the Bear says, "Only *you* can prevent forest fires." If conditions are right, dry and breezy, a carelessly discarded match or burning ash from a cigarette or cigar could destroy hundreds of acres of habitat.

If you smoke, save that Marlboro until you're in your car or at home.

48 — For quieter hunting, clean up your hunting area.

When you reach the spot where you plan to stand hunt, before settling down, take a few minutes to rake the immediate area clean of dry leaves and twigs. That way, nothing will crunch or crackle later on if you need to move around a little or maneuver for a clear shot.

49 — Hunt from a tree stand.

Deer and squirrels share the same habitat. A permanent tree stand can often do double-duty for both deer hunting *and* squirrel hunting. Similarly, you can set up a portable stand quickly in any squirrel hunting hotspots.

Hunting squirrels from a tree stand is not only quieter, since you won't be moving around much, but its height above the ground puts you more on level with your targets and shortens your shooting distance.

50 — Don't neglect late season squirrel hunting.

You may be tempted to forsake squirrel hunting late in the season when other hunting seasons open. But, remember, the late season squirrel hunter wins the bonus of tender, young spring- and summer-born squirrels.

And, because hunting seasons for other game animals do overlap squirrel season in many states, the late season hunter has the opportunity to do some 'mixed bag' hunting, too.

If you usually hunt with a shotgun, the same shot size you use for squirrels can be equally effective on rabbits and grouse. Or, carry a few rifled slugs along with the shot shells and you may be able to put some venison in your freezer alongside some dressed squirrels and rabbits.

51 — Keep an eye — and an ear — on your back trail.

If a squirrel is intent on foraging or searching for nuts it has cached — and if you remain very still and quiet while on stand — sometimes it may approach your position from behind, unaware of your presence.

If this happens, don't make any sudden movements and don't move toward the squirrel; let the squirrel close the distance to you. Turn slowly toward the sound and stop moving if the squirrel stops. The squirrel may be very near to you before it recognizes any danger and seeks refuge in a tree, affording you a close-range shot.

52 — Look for part of a squirrel.

Don't always expect to see a scared squirrel jumping from branch to branch to get away from you.

Sometimes, when frightened, a squirrel will simply hunker down and freeze in position, flattening itself against the tree trunk or branch, and wait for you to go away. If this happens, you may not be able to see the squirrel's whole body. Instead, look for just *a part* of it, such as its head or flicking tail. Look for any lump or bump that seems suspicious or looks out of place and wait for it to move. And, always, before you shoot, make sure the lump or bump that has drawn your attention *is* a squirrel and not just part of the tree. It's often easy to mistake the stub of a broken limb or a clump of leaves for a squirrel, if a squirrel is what you *expect* or *hope* to see.

Be patient, wait for it to move, be certain of your target before taking the shot.

53 — Use diversion to get an open shot.

Squirrels are canny creatures. But you can outsmart them.

If you're hunting alone and a squirrel keeps moving to the opposite side of the tree away from you, divert its attention.

Stand still and toss a stick or rock to the squirrel's side of the tree; the noise and movement often will scare the squirrel back around to your side of the tree where you can get a clear shot.

54 — Aim for a kill zone.

The only thing worse than missing a shot is hitting the squirrel but only wounding it.

Learn the kill zones of a squirrel and always try to place your bullet or shot in the right place to ensure a quick, humane kill with minimal damage to the meat.

The largest kill zone is the chest area. A shot to the chest from either the front or side (just behind the shoulder) will hit the heart, lungs and major arteries.

A smaller but equally vital zone is the head. Take this shot if the squirrel is playing hide-and-seek and all you can see is its head.

If you have a choice between taking a head shot or a chest shot, go for the chest.

It's easier to be selective with your shots if you use a rifle or pistol for hunting, but even if you normally hunt with a shotgun (which, of course, you have already patterned so that you know approximately what percentage of pellets will hit the target at a given range — see Tip #72) you can adjust your point of aim so that only a few pellets on the periphery of the shot pattern will find the kill zone. For a head shot, you can aim slightly in front of the head; for a chest shot, you may be able to aim at the head and feel confident that several pellets will strike the head and to a lesser extent the chest cavity.

Always avoid shooting at a squirrel that is facing away from you, especially if you're using a shotgun. A shot into a squirrel's rear end is less likely to be a killing shot, and it puts the pellets into the hind legs and back where most of the choice cuts of meat are located. A shot from behind may wound the squirrel and knock it out of the tree, but it still may be able to get away from you and hide; then you are ethically obligated to expend time and effort to find the squirrel and put it out of its misery. It's better to wait for the squirrel to change position, or move to get a better angle on a kill zone, before shooting.

55 — Camp out.

One way to ensure that you reach your hotspot early while squirrel activity is at its peak is simply to set up camp near the area the evening before you plan to hunt and spend the night there.

Camping out can make distant, off-the-beaten-path hunting spots more accessible because it gives you more time for actually hunting. You can rise at the crack of dawn and almost immediately begin hunting at the same time the squirrels are starting to stir; you won't be spending an hour or two of prime hunting time just hiking in to your hunting area.

Just be sure that you camp far enough away, or that you are downwind, from the area you're planning to hunt so that the smoke from your breakfast camp fire, if you make one, doesn't alarm your quarry. Speaking of fire, before you camp on public land, check first to make sure that an open campfire is allowed. Obtain a fire permit, if one is required. You may need to use a small backpacking stove if you want to fix a hot meal or a cup of coffee.

Even on private land, always observe some basic fire safety rules (after first getting the landowner's permission to have a campfire):

• Clear the area of your campfire of any combustible materials.

• Contain your campfire in a pit, preferably surrounded by rocks.

• Never leave your fire unattended.

• When you put out your campfire, douse it with water, stir the coals and ashes, and douse it again until all embers have been extinguished

56 — Wear camouflage.

Camouflage clothing is great for squirrel hunting. It helps you to meld with your surroundings and, combined with stealth, get closer to your quarry. But the danger of being shot by a careless hunter because of your 'invisibility' should not be ignored. Be safe; wear some 'hunter orange' clothing while in the woods.

A good compromise between the muted shades of full camouflage and solid orange apparel is the orange camouflage hunting clothing that's available now. Other hunters can readily see the bright, unnatural color, but the random pattern still breaks up your outline to help you fool sharp-sighted squirrels.

When hunting on public land a hunter orange cap, vest or jacket is required. On private land, where orange clothing is optional and not mandated by law, it is still a good idea if other hunters may be sharing the woods with you.

57 — Layer your clothing to meet changing conditions.

Temperature and weather often change quickly, and sometimes drastically, over the course of a hunting day.

Whether you are hunting in the fall or in the spring, the day may start out cool, even nippy, and warm up by midday to near summertime temperatures. A heavy coat or a rain jacket worn over a T-shirt and jeans may keep you comfortable while you're hunting early in the day in a chilly mist or fog. But, later, as the fog lifts and the air starts to warm, a coat or jacket may be more than you need, but just a shirt may be too little for comfort.

What do you do?

Simple: Wear layers of clothing, and shed a layer at a time as the day warms or the weather conditions change.

Start with underwear that wicks away perspiration. Next, add a layer for warmth. Depending on the weather and air temperature, wear a shirt made from a light- or heavy-weight wool or a wool blend fabric; pants should also be made of wool, wool blend or an insulating synthetic material. (Wool is an excellent insulator when dry and retains much of its insulating ability when wet. Avoid cotton or cotton blends; when wet, cotton quickly robs your body of heat.) Over your shirt wear a wool sweater, a down vest or a vest filled with synthetic insulation material. Your final layer should be a coat or jacket that provides warmth and blocks wind. And, if the weather is also damp, your final outer layer should be waterproof. Coats and jackets made with Gore-Tex® membrane and Thinsulate™ or similar insulating material are well worth their cost; they provide warmth, block wind *and* keep you dry. The *micro* pores in the Gore-Tex® material keep water droplets from penetrating but allow excess heat and water vapor from perspiration to escape.

And don't forget about your feet, hands and head.

Your feet will stay warmer in cold weather and cooler in hot weather if you wear a pair of lightweight inner socks to wick away perspiration, and heavier, preferably wool, socks over them to absorb the perspiration and provide insulation. If you hunt often in very cold weather, insulated hunting boots are a worthwhile investment.

Wear gloves to keep your ringers warm and flexible. After all, it's hard to make an accurate shot if your trigger finger is cold and stiff. Here again, layering is important. Plain leather gloves may protect your hands from scratches but they do little for keeping your hands warm. Wear gloves with a built-in insulating layer or wear a pair of wool gloves inside your plain leather gloves.

Finally, no matter the weather or time of year, always wear a cap or hat. In cool weather, a head cover of some kind helps you stay warm (you lose a lot of body heat through the top of your head). In warm weather, a hat or cap can help keep you cool by shading the top of your head from the sun and by soaking up perspiration, which then evaporates, cooling your head, and your body, in the process.

Layering also can help moderate your body temperature

during periods of activity and inactivity. Exertion — climbing a steep hillside or hurrying to your favorite hunting spot, for example — can cause you to overheat and break into a sweat, even in cold weather. Remove a layer or two of clothing when your activity level is high. When you slow down or stop to rest or stand hunt, put the sweater or jacket back on to avoid getting chilled. Heavy perspiration is especially dangerous in extremely cold weather because it can freeze into a thin coating of ice on your body, which rapidly lowers your core body temperature. Result: Hypothermia.

The layers of clothing you remove during the hunting day can be put back on again when the temperature takes a downward turn during the course of the day or as evening approaches, or when you stop to rest or settle down to wait for a squirrel to show itself.

58 — Wear 'quiet' clothing.

Wear clothing made of soft fabrics to reduce the noise of scraping against brush as you walk.

Nylon and many other synthetic materials 'sing' or 'whisper' when you walk or brush against bushes or tree limbs. Clothes made of natural fibers, especially wool, are better choices; they are soft and quiet.

59 — Don't *clink, rattle or jingle* when you move.

Squirrels have excellent hearing. If you cause extraneous noise when you walk, they will hear you coming and run off or hide long before you can spot them.

So, carry your extra ammunition in a looped cartridge

belt, or some other way that prevents the cartridges or shells from rattling or clinking together when you move. And don't carry any loose change in your pockets when you hunt. Leave it at home or in your vehicle. Why do you need it, anyway? There are no vending machines in the woods! And, if your rifle or shotgun is equipped with a sling, wrap the buckles or swivels with tape to minimize noise.

60 — Still hunt from a road.

For a less strenuous day of squirrel hunting, try hunting along a road if any run through your hunting area. This makes stalking, or still hunting, much quieter.

But don't shoot at a squirrel while you're actually *on* the road and don't shoot at a squirrel on the other side of the road. Shooting from or across a public road is illegal.

61 — Still hunt from a boat or canoe.

Drifting down a slow moving river or creek in a boat or canoe is often a productive way to hunt squirrels.

The banks of streams often are some of the most productive hunting areas. Some of squirrels' most favorite mast trees grow there, and the streams provide a dependable source of water. In addition, some streambeds are so wet and muddy, and the trees and brush so thick, that many hunters ignore these areas. When hunting pressure is light or non-existent, squirrels are less wary and easier prey.

62 — Silence your boat for float hunting.

Hunting from a boat is much quieter than tromping

through the woods. But some boats and canoes are quieter than others.

A boat or canoe made wood, or even fiberglass, is less noisy than one made of aluminum.

But if an aluminum boat is all you have, you can make it 'stealthier' by placing old carpeting in the bottom and padding the oars to deaden noise.

And, no matter what kind of boat you have, you won't be able to sneak up on many squirrels if you use a gasoline-powered outboard motor. Instead, use oars or a paddle to propel and steer your boat. Or, if that's a little more exercise than you like, use a trolling motor — the soft *whir* of the electric motor is barely noticeable more than a few feet away

63 — Shoot only at squirrels you can retrieve.

When you are float hunting, try to shoot squirrels that will not fall into the water.

A dead squirrel sometimes will pop back to the surface and float long enough to be picked up, but usually a shot squirrel that drops into the water will quickly sink and be lost. What a waste!

64 — Try to see the squirrel before it sees you.

The float hunter should stay close to the bank of the stream and drift around bends on the inside.

Squirrels are sharp-sighted; if you stay in the middle of the stream, most likely you won't surprise many squirrels. They'll spot your movement first and run off or hide. Stay close to the shoreline and use any available cover to mask your movement.

65 — Hunt with a partner.

A hunting partner can improve your chances for a productive hunt.

It's frustrating indeed to scare a squirrel into a tree but be unable to get a clear shot because as you move around the tree the little bushy-tailed rascal moves too, always keeping itself on the far side.

But if this happens while you're hunting with a partner it's easy to create a diversion that can force the squirrel into the open: One of you can circle the tree, somewhat noisily, while the other remains still. Then, when the squirrel moves back around to the side of the tree where the other hunter is waiting quietly — BANG!

And the *camaraderie* and fellowship of simply sharing the hunt with a friend is immeasurable.

66 — Carry a shotgun and a rifle.

When hunting with another person, it's often helpful for one of you to carry a shotgun and for the other to use a .22 caliber rifle.

The shotgunner can take the shots at running or jumping targets; the rifle can be used for long- or short-range still shots.

67 — Hunt with a squirrel dog.

A good squirrel dog can be a welcome companion while

hunting and a big help locating and treeing squirrels, and retrieving shot squirrels from heavy underbrush.

What breed of dog makes the best squirrel dog?

Well, a lot of good squirrel dogs are actually mixed breed. You know, the 'Heinz 57' variety — mutts. They might look like terriers, or long-legged gangly hounds; they might be long-haired, short-haired, scruffy or sleek, large or small...

But regardless of their physical appearance or undocumented parentage, good squirrel dogs all share similar characteristics: They have a natural instinct for finding and chasing and treeing squirrels; they are sharp-sighted with keen hearing and a discriminating sense of smell; they possess the ability to use all of their senses in the pursuit of squirrels; they are tough and brave, with no quit or back-up in them; and they don't mind mixing it up with a wounded squirrel and dispatching the critter for you.

If you have never hunted with a dog, but think you might enjoy it, find yourself a promising pup, train it or have it trained, and take it hunting with you. A good dog can add a new and exciting dimension to the sport.

68 — Choose a dog bred for squirrel hunting.

If you don't want to take your chances that a mixed breed pup from the local animal shelter has what it takes to be a good squirrel dog, consider buying a dog that has been bred specifically for its squirrel hunting ability. Check the Internet for breeders.

The National Kennel Club has recognized several breeds, strains and bloodlines as squirrel dogs. These include the American Squirrel Dog (a fairly recent NKC addition), Original Mountain Cur, Mountain Cur, Treeing Cur, Canadian Cur, Leopard Cur, Treeing Tennessee Brindles, Stephens Cur, Southern Blackmouth Cur, Blackmouth Cur, Henderson Cur, Camus Cur, Catahoula Cur, Mountain View Cur, Treeing Feist, Barger Stock Feist, Denmark Feist, Mullins Feist, Thornburg Feist, Cajun Squirrel Dog, West Siberian Laika, Rat Terrier, Jack Russell Terrier, Fox Terrier, German Jagdterrier, Airedale Terrier, Treeing Farm Shepherd, Norwegian Elkhound, Finnish Spitz, Walker Hound, English Hound, Bluetick Hound, Redbone Hound, and Black and Tan Hound. Each one has its own traits and qualities, and many perform equally well hunting other game, such as raccoons, opossums and wild boar, in addition to squirrels.

69 — Select a gun that is right for you.

The gun you choose to hunt squirrels depends generally on how, where and when you hunt.

If you normally still hunt, many of the squirrels you encounter will be moving, so a shotgun would be your best bet. If stand hunting is your preferred hunting method, an accurate .22 rimfire rifle can be a more productive weapon.

A .22 can often be used more effectively than a shotgun if you usually hunt in open woodland, where squirrels can be targeted at a fairly long range, or if you're after fox squirrels that are foraging in an open, harvested field. A smoothbore, on the other hand, can prove its value in dense, brushy terrain where squirrels move quickly in and out of cover and shots are made at relatively short range and shot placement doesn't have to be precise.

If you do most of your hunting in the spring season or early in the fall when the trees are leafy and opportunities for open shots are rare, using a shotgun loaded with heavy shot can bust through the foliage and get past small limbs that could deflect a small caliber bullet. This is not to say that you can't or shouldn't use a rifle under these conditions, but you may have to hunt harder and be satisfied with fewer squirrels. A .22 can be employed effectively when trees are bare, and stalking becomes more difficult and shooting distances get longer.

Personal preference is also an important factor in weapon choice. When all is said and done, the best hunting weapon is the one you're used to, the one with which you're most comfortable and most skilled.

Rifle or shotgun—it's up to you.

70 — Choose the best shotgun action and gauge.

Just about any type and gauge of shotgun can be used for squirrel hunting—single-shot, bolt action, pump or semi-automatic in .410-, 28-, 20-, 16-, or 12-gauge. (A 10-gauge shotgun, normally used for knocking down high-flying geese, however, is probably a bit too much gun for squirrels in most situations; and 28- and 16-gauge guns aren't as popular as they once were and ammo for them is harder to find.)

The single-shot shotgun probably has killed more squirrels than all other types of shotguns combined. Many hunters use a single-shot exclusively for squirrel hunting, either because that's the gun they started using when they were young and are more comfortable with it, or because using a single-shot action adds another degree of difficulty and challenge to an already difficult and challenging sport. Or because it is very affordable — a single-shot is much simpler in construction and operation and, therefore, less expensive than a pump or semi-auto, or even a bolt-action shotgun.

A bolt-action shotgun is a step up from the single-shot. It offers dependability on par with a single-shot, as well as the advantage of a magazine-fed repeating action for fairly quick follow-up shots. Bolt actions are not as a popular as they once were and are not seen much anymore, but they are still excellent squirrel guns.

More and more hunters today are using a pump, or slide-action, shotgun because of its ease of handling and magazine capacity...and its versatility. Most pump shotguns allow you to interchange different length and different choke barrels, so that the same gun can be used to hunt different game.

A semi-automatic shotgun can also be used, of course. And if that's what you have, use it. But it's probably not the best choice for a young hunter who needs to learn marksmanship and fire discipline.

As for gauge, which is the best for squirrel hunting?

Actually, there probably is no *best* shotgun gauge for squirrel hunting. It all comes down to personal preference and skill. The diminutive .410 can be used just as effectively as the 12- or 20-gauge. The important thing is to know your shotgun, know its virtues and shortcomings, its strengths and limitations, its advantages and disadvantages.

71 — Choose the best choke for your shotgun

Shotgun barrels come in various chokes for different types of hunting.

Choke refers to the amount of constriction in the bore of a shotgun barrel to control the concentration of pellets. The more constriction, which begins about three inches from the muzzle, the more concentrated the shot pellets during flight; less constriction produces a wider spread of pellets in the same distance.

Chokes on shotguns range from Full, which has the greatest constriction and, therefore, produces the densest shot pattern, to Cylinder, which means no choke at all, i.e., the bore is the maximum diameter the whole length of the barrel. A shotgun with a Cylinder bore is ideal for home defense, where you want a wide pattern at close range to ensure that you hit your target (such as some miscreant intent on evil-doing) with at least some of the pellets; but it is less than ideal for squirrel hunting. Between Full Choke and Cylinder Choke, other popular chokes are Improved Modified, Modified, Improved Cylinder, and Skeet.

The most popular chokes for squirrel hunting are Full Choke, for the little 410-gauge, and Modified Choke for the 12- and 20-gauge guns.

If the only shotgun available to you for hunting has a

Cylinder bore, you can improve its utility and versatility by fitting it with a variable choke, which will allow you to 'dial in' the choke you desire.

72 — Pattern your shotgun before hunting.

Unfortunately, you can't always rely on what is marked on the barrel to determine the choke of your shotgun. Choke often varies from gun maker to gun maker. Two 12-gauge shotguns, for example, both stamped Modified Choke but each made by a different manufacturer, may shoot very different patterns.

The only way to know the actual choke of your shotgun for certain is *to pattern* it.

Choke is determined by the percentage of pellets from a particular shotgun shell load that strikes within a 30-inch circle at 40 yards. To pattern your shotgun, draw a bullseye in the center of a piece of paper about 40 inches square, then draw a 30-inch diameter circle around the bullseye. Set the target up 40 yards away, aim at the bullseye and fire. Check the target and count the number of holes within the circle. Divide the number of hits inside the circle by the total pellets in the shotgun shell to arrive at a percentage. Then compare this figure to the choke table to determine the choke. For example, if the shotgun shell you're shooting contains 27 #4 pellets and 21 of the pellets hit within the circle, simply divide 21 by 27 and you get .77, or 77-percent. Compare this percentage to the table and you'll see that the pattern falls within the Full Choke range.

Okay, now you know that the barrel on the shotgun

you're using may say Modified, but in actuality it is throwing a Full Choke pattern at standard shotgun range.

Choke	% of shot in 30" circle @ 40 yards
Full Choke	70-80%
Improved Modified	65-70%
Modified	55-65%
Quarter Choke	50-55%
Improved Cylinder	45-50%
Cylinder	35-40%

Patterning your shotgun so that you know exactly what pattern it shoots is just as important as sighting in a rifle. If you know your shotgun's actual choke and pick your shots accordingly, you will have fewer misses and fewer crippled squirrels.

73 — For shotgun hunting, use the proper shot size.

If you normally hunt squirrels with a shotgun, use heavier shot in the early fall when leaves are on the trees, lighter shot later in the season when the leaves have mostly fallen or squirrels are on the ground.

Preferences vary among hunters, of course, but generally #4 shot is considered a bit heavy for squirrels and #8 shot a bit too light. Which leaves #5, #6, and #7-1/2 to choose from.

Use #5 shot for penetrating heavy foliage, #7-1/2 for

when the trees are bare. If you want to keep things simple and stick to just one standard load, then #6 is a good all-purpose shot size.

And save the 'magnum' shotgun shells with heavy pellet loads for duck and goose season. High-velocity standard load shells are more than enough for squirrels.

74 — Choose a .22 for your squirrel rifle.

The .22-caliber long rifle cartridge is arguably the best cartridge for taking squirrels.

The standard velocity round with solid 40-grain bullet, if placed properly, is more than sufficient for dispatching squirrels quickly and efficiently. At most normal ranges, it has enough energy to penetrate, but not so much *umph* that it simply zips through the squirrel without causing lethal tissue damage.

Some hunters make a case for using hollow point bullets, which they claim ensures a surer kill because of expansion and deformation of the bullet when it strikes flesh; however, expansion of a standard velocity .22-caliber hollow point is negligible, and for most intents and purposes a solid lead bullet is just as deadly.

What *kind* of .22 rimfire rifle should you use?

Well, for the utmost in accuracy and dependability, a single shot rifle or bolt-action repeater is hard to beat. Which is not to say that if what you have to hunt with is a semi-auto, don't use it. In the right hands, practically any modern semi-automatic .22 available today is still capable of better accuracy than most hunters can muster even with a single shot Olympic-style target rifle. The key is to practice with what you have to become as proficient and as accurate as possible, so that your first shot is a killing shot.

The 'disadvantage' of using a semi-auto .22 rifle is the same as for a semi-auto action shotgun: If the hunter is not already disciplined enough to always strive to make the first shot count, a semi-auto can encourage the hunter to rely heavily on making the killing shot with the second or third, or fourth or fifth, round, which is so easily available by just pulling the trigger again.

[Somehow I recognized this fact early and, although the only 'squirrel gun' I owned when I was a youngster was an older, well used .22 semi-auto, I often went into the woods in search of squirrels with only a round in the chamber, an empty magazine and a small handful of extra cartridges in my pocket. In other words, I treated that semi-auto like a single shot rifle even though the magazine would hold ten or 11 .22 long rifle cartridges, because I understood without really being told that having only one shot would make me a better shot.]

75 — Get on target quicker with the right sights.

On a rifle with open sights, a red or white front bead or post sight shows up better in dim light.

If your squirrel gun isn't equipped this way already, install a high visibility front sight or paint the front sight white or red for quicker, more accurate aiming.

76 — Get 'closer' to your quarry with a telescopic sight.

A telescopic sight is a wise investment for a .22-caliber squirrel rifle.

Good quality optics can help you locate a squirrel hidden in the branches in the top of a tree and allow you to place your shot in a kill zone with precision, which is sometimes difficult to manage with open sights.

Just make sure that you equip your squirrel rifle with the right kind of scope.

There has been a trend in recent years to mount higher power scopes made for big game and varmint rifles on .22-caliber rimfires in the belief that the higher powered, higher priced and, supposedly, higher quality optics offer a brighter sight picture and greater accuracy than scopes made specifically for use on rimfires or air rifles. Some of these trendy shooters are often surprised to find that their accuracy rate can actually decline when using big game scopes on .22's, Despite the 'advantages' of the big game optics, they begin missing easy shots because they failed to allow for the excessive *parallax* that occurs when big game scopes are used at normal rimfire ranges.

Parallax is a condition that occurs in all telescopic sights if the reticle, or crosshairs, inside the scope is not exactly parallel to the image plane. This makes the shooter's eye position a critical factor in obtaining consistent accuracy with a scope. In other words, if the shooter is looking through the scope at the crosshairs from even a slight angle rather than straight-on and aligned with the optics, the sight picture he gets will differ slightly from what the scope and, therefore, the rifle is actually pointed at. This difference is more pronounced in big game scopes, which are generally corrected for parallax, or 'focused' to be parallax-free, by the factory at 150 yards, while the correction for rimfire scopes is usually 50 yards.

One solution is to send the scope back to the factory with instructions to reset the parallax to 50 yards. Another is to buy a (more expensive) scope with a parallax adjustment feature that allows the shooter the set the desired range correction.

The best solution, however, is simply to avoid the problem entirely. Purchase a good quality scope made for .22 rimfires. A 4-power (4X) scope with a 25mm or 30mm lens is a good choice for squirrel hunters. It provides a wide angle of view, which makes it easier to follow a moving squirrel, and the larger lens gathers more light and provides a brighter sight picture in low-light conditions.

77— Hunt with a handgun.

To add more excitement and challenge, hunt squirrels with a .22-caliber handgun.

Either a revolver or a semi-auto pistol can be used with equal effectiveness. Just remember to practice your marksmanship first.

And make sure a handgun is a legal hunting weapon in your state or in the area you plan to hunt.

78 — For nearly silent shooting, pellet-ize squirrels.

Air rifles, or pellet guns, have become very popular with a number of squirrel hunters, and for good reason.

They are extremely quiet, which is a particularly attractive feature for squirrel hunting. And, with a commercial or even a homemade pellet trap, you can target practice in your basement or in your backyard without disturbing your family or neighbors.

And because pellets fired from air rifles have less energy and lower velocity than most .22-caliber cartridges or shotgun shells, you can even do some silent hunting in your backyard without a lot of concern that a miss or a ricochet will create a problem with your neighbors. A .22 bullet can travel up to a mile, and a ricochet almost as far. A pellet can travel a few hundred feet at best, and since a sub-sonic pellet from an air rifle transfers most of its energy on initial contact a ricochet will drop harmlessly to the ground after a short distance.

Air rifles offer a number of other advantages, too.

Unlike regular rifles, handguns and shotguns, you can buy a high-quality adult air rifle without any kind of permit or paperwork in most states, and you can buy it by mail order or over the Internet and have it shipped directly to your home.

In terms of quality, features and price, you have a lot to choose from. Manufacturers such as RWS, Beeman, Daisy, Baikal, CZ and a few others produce high quality air rifles that are rugged enough and accurate enough to use hunting squirrels. Many feature adjustable triggers, adjustable stocks and a choice of sights; most will accept the installation of a telescopic sight, which would be a valuable addition for squirrel hunting. You have several power options to choose from, too — CO_2, pre-charged pneumatic, multiple-pump for variable velocity and energy, and single-shot break barrels. You also have several caliber options nowadays. Although the most common pellet calibers are still .177 (BB) and .22, many manufacturers are now offering air rifles in .20 caliber,

.25-caliber, 9mm, and even .50-caliber.

Ammunition for air rifles is cheap; even match grade .22-caliber pellets are quite affordable, similar in price to the same quantity of standard velocity, non-match grade .22-caliber rimfire cartridges.

A final advantage is weight. Although many of the match grade target-style air rifles weigh as much as their rimfire counterparts, many popular air rifles that are ideal for squirrel hunting may weigh only half as much as a .22 rifle or a shotgun.

79 — Make an 'over/under' your squirrel gun.

Because of its versatility, an over/under rifle/shotgun in .22-caliber/12-, 20-, or even .410-ga. is an excellent all-around gun for the squirrel hunter.

You can use the rifle barrel for long- or short-range still shots; the shotgun barrel can be used for running shots.

Of course, you only get one shot from each barrel without reloading; but if you've done your target practice during the pre-season, one shot from either barrel is all you need. Right?

80 — Know your weapon's effective range.

For consistent success hunting squirrels it is imperative to know the effective range of the gun you're using and to judge distances reasonably accurately so that you only take shots within that range.

Although a .22 caliber bullet can travel up to a mile and

a load of shotgun pellets from a standard velocity shell can travel several hundred yards, these are maximum, not effective, ranges. Effective range refers to the longest distance at which you can expect that particular rifle, pistol or shotgun to produce an accurate and killing shot.

At 60 or 70 yards you *may* be able to hit a squirrel with *a few* shotgun pellets, but it is highly unlikely that enough pellets will strike the squirrel with enough force or energy to penetrate its tough skin and produce a lethal wound. A shotgun hunter should know that a squirrel is out of range at more than 40 yards. Similarly, a .22-caliber bullet fired from a rifle may not have enough energy past 100 yards to produce consistent kills; 50 or 60 yards is probably its maximum effective range. And, because of its shorter barrel and sight plane, a .22-caliber handgun's effective range is considerably less; shots at a range of more than 25 yards probably shouldn't even be attempted. Most squirrels are taken at a range of ten yards to 60 yards.

If a squirrel is outside your weapon's effective range when you first spot it, work yourself closer to it or wait for it to move closer to you before taking your shot.

81— Know *your* effective range.

Your effective range is usually much less than your weapon's effective range.

You may be consistently accurate with your squirrel rifle out to 100 yards when you are at the firing range and shooting from a bench rest at a stationary target, but shooting out in the woods at an unpredictable and quick-moving target like a squirrel is something else entirely.

If you are confident of hitting your target every time at 50 yards or less, don't waste a shot or risk merely wounding a squirrel that you judge to be 75 yards away

Know your limitations. Know your effective range.

82 — Use support to improve your aim.

Always take advantage of any available support to steady your aim, no matter whether you're hunting with a rifle, a handgun, or even a shotgun. Use a tree trunk, use a sapling (if there's no wind), or shoot from a sitting position and use your knees for support. A hiking staff can also do double-duty as a monopod to help you stabilize your aim.

Never shoot offhand if there is something close by to use for support.

83 — Shoot and...wait.

If you kill a squirrel with a rifle or pistol, note where it falls and remain still for a few minutes.

The report of a .22 often will not disturb other squirrels in the area for long and you may be able to bag a second squirrel without moving from your original shooting position.

84 — For more challenge, bow hunt for squirrels.

If you bow hunt deer, bow hunting squirrels can be even more challenging.

Shooting the small, darting targets with an arrow requires skill and practice; but a successful hit, even at a range of only 10 or 15 yards, is a gratifying and confidence-building experience.

Save the broad heads for deer. For bow hunting squirrels, leave the broad heads at home and use arrows with points made specifically for small game.

Several types are available for the small game bow hunter, including blunt tips that bludgeon rather than pierce, barb-less field points, short barbed collars that fit behind a field point and give the arrow some grip in the target, and wire prong points. There are even 'points' with wide looped wire heads, so that if you 'miss' by a couple of inches you can still score a hit.

86 — Aim low to save your arrows.

Avoid high angle shots whenever possible.

A missed shot can travel a long distance and it's almost impossible to track its flight to the ground for later recovery. Too often the result is a missed squirrel and a lost arrow *and* a lot of wasted hunting time spent searching for it.

If you use the same type of arrow for squirrels that you use for deer, pass up the shots at squirrels high in the trees. Go after squirrels on or near the ground. A missed shot or a shot that completely penetrates a squirrel's body won't travel very far.

87 — Use short-range arrows for squirrels.

If you would rather not limit yourself only to low-angle targets when bow hunting for squirrels, use arrows with 'flu-flu' fletching to prevent the arrows from traveling too far if you miss.

Target arrows and arrows made for hunting large game use three trimmed fletches, or feather vanes, to stabilize the arrow in flight. This minimal fletching results in low air resistance and, consequently, high velocity and long range. Flu-flu arrows, on the other hand, are fletched with five or six full-length feathers or two to four fluffy feathers wrapped around the arrow shaft, which increase air resistance and impede the arrow's flight. Originally designed for shooting at flying targets, flu-flu arrows fly fast and straight for about 20 yards, then quickly slow down and fall to the ground.

88 — Don't try to pick up a wounded squirrel.

Squirrels have sharp teeth and extremely powerful jaws — they can chew through or crack nut hulls, remember. And their hooked claws are needle-sharp. Even if seriously wounded, they can inflict a painful bite and deep puncture wounds and scratches.

And they're tenacious critters. If they bite or if they hook their claws in you, they don't want to let go.

[Another hunting partner of mine can attest to this.

He had knocked a fox squirrel out of a tall oak tree, but neither the shot nor the fall killed it. As soon as the squirrel hit the ground it *bolted for a hole in the base of the tree trunk. Caught up in the excitement, my partner sprinted to the tree and thrust his unprotected hand into the hole and began groping for the squirrel.*

Well, he found it!

Or maybe it would be more accurate to say it found him!

With a yowl, he jerked his hand out of the hole. And clamped onto one finger was that squirrel! Flinging his arm up and down, back and forth, he tried to shake the squirrel loose. Then he tried to pull the squirrel off. But that bushy-tail was hurt and scared and literally hanging on for dear life.

It took a couple of good solid whacks up against the tree trunk to stun the squirrel so that he could remove it from his mangled finger.]

The lesson, of course, is: Don't try to grab or pick up a wounded squirrel with your bare hand.

If a shot squirrel crawls into a hole in the ground or a hollow tree trunk, use a stick to roust it out. Never, ever, reach in after it with your bare hand.

Sometimes, of course, there is no other way to retrieve a wounded squirrel except to reach in and grab it. It's not sporting or ethical to leave it to suffer and die.

So, include a pair of heavy leather gloves in your hunting gear. Then, if you must handle a wounded squirrel, put on the gloves first.

89 — Be sure of your kill.

After retrieving a shot squirrel, check carefully to make sure it's dead before stuffing it into the game pocket of your hunting jacket.

If the squirrel was just stunned by the wound or the fall,

it could regain consciousness after you pocket it. In that case, it is highly likely that it would be highly agitated, frantic, clawing to get out and away.

Make sure the squirrel has expired before you pick it up. A good way to do this is to get the squirrel in a facedown position, then step on the squirrel firmly to compress its chest against the ground for a minute or two. If the squirrel is not already dead, it will expire quickly and quietly without any meat loss.

90 – Get to a wounded squirrel quickly.

If you can see that your shot only wounded a squirrel, get to it quickly before it can crawl off and hide.

91– No plastic!

If you plan on shooting more than one squirrel, you're going to need a way to carry your harvest.

Some hunters use a plastic bag. It's lightweight, foldable and easily carried in your pocket until needed. But if the day is warm and you anticipate hunting more than a few hours, keeping squirrel carcasses in a plastic bag can hasten spoilage. Plastic doesn't 'breathe;' consequently, the squirrel carcasses will not cool very quickly and could go bad before you dress them out.

If your hunting jacket has a game pocket, you can use it. But be aware that keeping a dead squirrel in direct and prolonged contact with the heat from your body can also have an adverse effect on the freshness of the meat.

It may be better to use a cloth bag to ensure good airflow and to keep the squirrel carcasses as cool as possible while you work on limiting out. A cloth bag also will allow blood seeping from the carcasses to drain away. (Even if you cut a dead squirrel's jugular to bleed out the body, you can still get some seepage from the wounds.) By the end of the day's hunt, shot squirrels kept in a plastic bag could literally be floating in blood that has drained from the carcasses and pooled in the bottom of the bag. And this makes skinning and gutting a much messier job than it needs to be.

92 — Avoid infection.

Squirrels and other rodents, as well as rabbits and hares, are susceptible to an illness called tularemia.

This disease, caused by the bacterium *Frantiselta tularensis*, can be passed to humans if they handle infected animal carcasses, are bitten by an infected tick, deerfly or other insect, eat or drink contaminated food or water, or even inhale *F. tularensis* bacteria.

Tularemia is a serious disease; it can be fatal if not treated quickly with the right antibiotics. Symptoms, which usually appear in three to five days and as long as 14 days, include sudden fever, chills, headaches, muscle aches, joint pain, dry cough and progressive weakness.

Depending on how a person was exposed to the disease, other symptoms might include ulcers on the skin or mouth, swollen and painful lymph glands, swollen and painful eyes, and a sore throat. Persons infected with tularemia can also develop pneumonia, chest pain, and bloody sputum. They can have trouble breathing, and even stop breathing!

To protect yourself from contracting a disease such as tularemia or getting an infection through scratches or cuts in the skin, always wear some sort of protective gloves while field dressing or cleaning squirrels. It's a good idea to put a pair of rubber or vinyl kitchen gloves or a couple of pairs of latex surgical gloves in your hunting pack. Cloth gloves are not adequate. And wash your hands thoroughly with soap and water or a waterless anti-bacterial hand cleaner after handling a squirrel carcass.

To avoid insect bites that could transmit tularemia or other diseases use an insect repellent containing DEET.

When field dressing a squirrel, look for signs of tularemia (see Tip #95) and discard the squirrel if any are found.

And, of course, even squirrels that show no signs of disease and appear to be healthy should be thoroughly cooked before eating them.

93 — Gut squirrels as soon as possible after you bag them.

A freshly killed squirrel is much easier to gut and skin. The job becomes more difficult after the muscle tissue begins to stiffen.

But if you would rather wait until you're out of the woods before you start skinning and cutting up your harvest, that's all right. A dead squirrel generally will 'keep' all day while you're hunting if it is cooled quickly, kept out of the sun and has good air circulation around it.

Gutting the squirrel as soon as possible will help the cooling process. Most hunters don't want to lug around a cooler full of ice, which is understandable, but stuffing clean grass into the squirrel's body cavity can aid cooling and absorb blood.

94 — Quick cleaning can salvage a gut-shot squirrel.

If your aim is a little off and you gut-shoot a squirrel, it's especially important that you skin it and clean it as quickly as possible to preserve meat quality and flavor.

Nothing taints the flavor of squirrel — or the meat of any other game animal, for that matter — faster than urine and intestinal contents that are allowed to stay in contact with the muscle tissue.

After skinning and gutting, use some of your drinking water to rinse the body cavity and wash out any contamination, then pat dry.

Or, use water from a spring or creek in your hunting area. Don't worry about bacteria or parasites that may be in this untreated water. Rinsing again with potable water later when you get home, and proper cooking temperature and time when you prepare the squirrel for eating, will eliminate any possible danger.

95 — Clean a squirrel the right way.

The more care you take skinning, gutting and cutting up your squirrels, the better they will taste in your favorite recipes.

There are several 'right' ways to skin a squirrel, and they are all very similar. Which method you use depends on where you are doing the cleaning — in the field or at

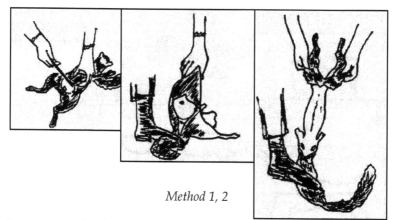

Method 1, 2

home—and what is easiest for you.

Skinning method #1—Make a diagonal cut at the base of the squirrel's hind legs from the tail to the belly Cut through the tailbone, but don't cut off the tail. Step on the tail, grasp the squirrel's hind legs with one hand, and pull. Most of the skin will come off with the tail. Skin the hind legs separately. Cut off the feet and head. Wash and pick off any loose hairs clinging to the carcass.

Skinning method #2—Cut the tail bone through from under the tail, leaving the tail attached to the skin, and continue the cut across the width of the back. Holding the hind legs, turn the squirrel over on its back, step on the base of the tail and pull up steadily and slowly until the skin has been peeled down over the front legs and head. Pull the remaining skin from the hind legs. Then cut off the head and feet. Again, get rid of any hair adhering to the carcass.

Skinning method #3— First, give the squirrel a thorough soaking in water to keep the fur matted down and to wash off any loose hair. Make a cut on the underside of the tail at the base, slicing through the tailbone but leaving the tail attached to the back skin. Extend the cut along the squirrel's flanks.

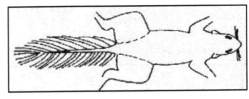

Step on the tail and pull up on the hind legs. Tug the skin over the fore legs and hind legs, then cut off the feet and head.

Skinning method #4 — This is probably the simplest method: Cut off the feet, head and tail first. Then cut a small slit across the back about midway on the squirrel's body. Work your fingers into the slit until you get a good grip and pull toward the front and the back until you get the skin down to the legs. Work the skin down the legs until it comes completely off in one piece. Wash or wipe off any hair sticking to the carcass.

Method 3

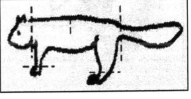

Method 4

No matter which skinning technique you use, there's really only one way to properly gut a squirrel: First, remove all the musk glands to prevent a bitter taste when the squirrel is cooked and eaten. These glands appear as small gray-colored balls found on the neck, under the front leg 'arm pits,' on the belly and hip areas, and directly behind the hind leg knee joints inside the flesh (you'll have to cut all the way to the bone to find and remove these). Lay the skinned squirrel on its back and cut down the center of the squirrel from one end to the other. Be careful not to cut too deeply and nick the entrails. Cut completely through the pelvic bone so the colon can be removed. Once the viscera are exposed, locate the liver and look for signs of tularemia (see Tip #92). If the squirrel is infected with tularemia, the liver will have white or yellow spots on it; if you see signs of this disease, discard the carcass. If the liver looks healthy, then look for the urinary bladder. If it appears to be full, pinch the neck of the bladder and cut to remove it. Getting rid of the bladder prevents any accidental 'squirts' during gutting that

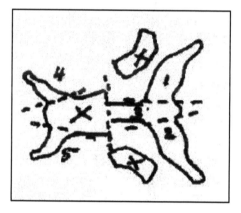

could taint the meat and require additional cleaning and 'decontamination' before cooking. Reach into the carcass behind the heart and pull out all the innards. Finally, rinse out the body cavity.

There are five, or six, choice cuts of squirrel meat. These are the four legs and the back (which contains the tenderloin). The sixth choice piece of squirrel, at least for some folks, is the head, which contains morsels of good meat on the cheeks and on the back of the head where it meets the back. And some hunters consider the little squirrel brain some-thing of a delicacy.

Remember, the care and effort you put into cleaning your squirrels properly will be amply rewarded with your first bite of pan-fried squirrel or squirrel potpie.

96 — Save the tail!

Some fishing tackle companies and many anglers who make their own flies and lures will buy them. Check the classified ads in outdoors magazines for buyers.

Most buyers will want the bone left in the tail, so keep this in mind when you field dress your squirrels.

97 — Prepare your squirrel correctly for cooking and eating.

Squirrel can be cooked immediately after cleaning without any additional preparation. Just make sure no hair is sticking to the carcass or squirrel pieces; if you took proper care during the skinning process, this should not be a problem.

But if you intend to cook it later in the day or the next day, place the dressed squirrel in a non-metallic container such as a plastic bowl or a gallon-size plastic zip bag with a mixture of about a gallon of water, 1/4 cup of salt and a couple of tablespoons of baking soda, and refrigerate. Rinse with plain water and pat dry before using it in your favorite squirrel dish.

For a gut-shot squirrel, rinse the squirrel and wash out the body cavity with a mixture of 1/4 cup of vinegar in about a gallon of water, and rinse with plain water and pat dry before cooking. Or, rinse with plain water before refrigerating it in the saltwater solution.

98 — Freeze squirrels for future meals.

If you do a lot of hunting and kill a lot of squirrels, most likely you won't want to eat fresh squirrel *every* day. If you don't plan on cooking the squirrel within 24 hours, then you need to freeze it for later use.

To freeze squirrels (or other small game, such as rabbits) cut a 3-inch hole in the top of a gallon milk jug; leave the handle attached. Put one or two cleaned squirrels into the jug and fill it with water. Use an indelible marker and write the date and contents on the jug. Then put the jug in your deep freeze. The meat will stay fresh for months, and there's no freezer burn.

If you own a vacuum sealer, you can vacuum package each individual squirrel (or meal-size portions) before freezing. Again, be sure to mark the date and contents on the package. With this method, too, there is little danger of freezer burn because most of the air is removed from the package before sealing. And, the vacuum-sealed packages take up a lot less space in your freezer.

99 — Always practice basic firearms safety...

• Treat every gun as if it were loaded.

• Be absolutely sure of your target; never shoot at sound or movement.

• Always keep the muzzle of your gun pointed in a safe direction.

• Never climb a tree or fence with a loaded firearm.

• Never point a gun anything you do not plan to shoot.

100 — ...and always observe the basic rules of ethical hunting.

• Get the landowner's permission before hunting on private land.

• Know the state laws that regulate squirrel hunting.

• Use the squirrels you harvest.

• Practice your marksmanship to ensure quick, humane kills.

• Learn to identify legal game.

• Keep game clean, dry, and cool.

101 — Keep the hunting tradition alive.

Squirrel hunting is a great way to pass on the hunting tradition and an appreciation of nature to the next generation.

Don't let hunting disappear. Share a hunt, share your woods craft, share your squirrel hunting knowledge with a youngster. Keep the tradition alive!

•••

Cooking Squirrels

• One squirrel = one hearty serving.

• Examine carcasses carefully to locate embedded shot and remove them with a sharp pointed knife.

• Wash off squirrels *before* cutting them into pieces.

• Squirrel can be prepared the same ways you prepare chicken and substituted in most chicken dishes – but squirrel doesn't taste like chicken! Squirrel is a medium red meat with a richer flavor than chicken.

• Old squirrels are tougher than young squirrels; more cooking time is needed to tenderize them.

• Use the best quality and freshest spices, herbs and other ingredients in your squirrel dishes – always.

• In recipes calling for wine, use only good quality wine that you'd actually drink. Leave the so called 'cooking' wines on the supermarket shelf.

• If you believe your dinner guests may be squeamish about eating 'tree rats,' simply tell them that you're preparing a special culinary treat, Sciurus Fricassee, a 'Latin' delicacy.

•••

Squirrel Recipes

The recipes in this section were collected over many years from a variety of sources. In many cases the origins of the recipes have been lost, and the recipes have been altered slightly and ingredients substituted, according to personal preference and taste.

For example, the original recipe for Pan Fried Squirrel came from the mother of one of my hunting buddies when I was a teenager. She often sent us off on our squirrel hunting excursions with some of her fried squirrel (and usually a piece of dried apple pie for each of us) wrapped in brown paper for our *al fresco* lunch in the woods. She depended on the wild game her son brought home to help feed the family, so she made sure we were well fortified for the hunt. She cooked with lard, and she fried the squirrel in melted lard. But since we worry a lot nowadays about cholesterol, vegetable oil has been substituted for lard in this recipe. Other recipes have undergone similar modifications.

In most things, cooking included, I believe in the KISS principle—Keep It Simple, Stupid! (or, to be 'politically correct,' Keep It Super Simple!). Often the simplest fare makes the best and most memorable meal. You'll find some plain-and-simple squirrel dishes in the following pages. But even though simpler is often better, to my way of thinking, I'm not averse to fancyin' up a squirrel dish if the occasion or mood calls for it. You'll find some fancy dishes here, too.

Pan-Fried Squirrel

4 young squirrels, cut up

Coating mixture:

All-purpose flour

Seasoned salt (a liberal amount)

Fresh ground black pepper

Vegetable oil

Dredge squirrel pieces in coating mixture. Pour enough cooking oil in a non-stick or well-seasoned cast iron skillet so that squirrel pieces will be immersed about half their thickness. Heat oil over medium to medium-high heat. When the oil is hot, brown the squirrel pieces on all sides. Avoid knocking off coating mixture when turning the pieces. When browned, reduce heat to medium-low, cover skillet and cook until pieces are fork tender, or about 30 minutes.

Fancy Fried Squirrel

2 dressed young squirrels, cut in pieces

2 tablespoons extra virgin olive oil

1 large onion, sliced thin

1 cup water

1 tablespoon dry sage

2 cloves minced garlic

1 teaspoon dry basil

1 teaspoon dry parsley

1 cup red wine

In a heavy skillet, heat oil over medium heat. Add squirrel pieces and cook, turning occasionally until evenly browned, about 10 minutes.

Add all other ingredients except wine, reduce heat to low, and cover. Simmer for 1 to 1-1/2 hours, or until meat is tender.

Add wine and continue to cook, uncovered, over medium heat for another 10 minutes.

Broiled Squirrel

4 squirrels, cut up in large sections

4 teaspoons salt

1 teaspoon pepper

2 teaspoons cooking oil

Rub squirrels with salt and pepper mixture. Brush with oil and place on rack in roasting pan. Broil 40 minutes, basting every 10 minutes with drippings. Serves 4.

Squirrel Fricassee

2 dressed young squirrels cut in pieces

1/2 cup all-purpose flour

1 1/2 tsp. salt

Pepper

1/2 cup vegetable shortening

1/4-3/4 cup water

1 -1-1/2 cups milk

1 teaspoon grated onion

Wipe squirrels thoroughly with a damp cloth and remove any hair still clinging to the carcass. Wash thoroughly inside and out with lukewarm water. Drain, pat dry, and cut into serving pieces.

Combine salt, pepper and flour; dredge squirrel pieces in the mixture. Heat shortening in a heavy skillet over medium heat; brown meat slowly on all sides to a rich brown (about 15 minutes). Add 1/4 cup of the water, cover, reduce heat to low and simmer, adding more water as needed, about 30-45 minutes. Squirrel should be very tender when done. Remove squirrel to a hot platter; cover and keep hot.

To make gravy, stir the remaining flour mixture into the hot liquid in the skillet and add the milk and grated onion. Heat the mixture until it boils and begins to thicken, stirring constantly. When the gravy reaches the desired consistency, remove from heat and serve immediately with the squirrel.

Baked Squirrel

4 squirrels, cleaned

Flour

Salt

Pepper

1 cup water

1/4 cup Worcestershire Sauce

2 tablespoons chopped parsley

1 clove of garlic, minced

1 small bay leaf

Mix flour, salt and pepper; dredge squirrels in mixture. Brown in roasting pan. Mix remaining ingredients and pour over squirrels. Bake at 350° for 45 minutes. Reduce temperature to 300° and continue cooking about 45 minutes, until tender.

Broiled Squirrel

Clean squirrels and rub with salt and pepper. Brush with oil and place on hot broiling rack. Broil 40 minutes, turning and basting with drippings every 10 minutes. Serve with gravy made from drippings and flour seasoned with 1 -2 tablespoons lemon juice.

Dutch Oven Squirrel

Cut up squirrels. Dredge pieces in a mixture of flour, dash of ginger, salt, and pepper. Brown on all sides in oil. Put browned squirrel in large, heavy Dutch oven. Add 3/4 cup hot water; cover and put in 325 degrees oven for 2 hours or until tender.

Sautéed Squirrel

2 young squirrels, cut up

2 tablespoons extra virgin olive oil

1 medium onion, chopped

1 medium bell pepper, chopped

1 clove garlic, minced

1/2 teaspoon oregano

1/4 teaspoon mace

1/4 teaspoon ground cloves

1/2 cup dry white wine

1/2 pound fresh mushrooms

2 tablespoons butter

1/2 cup tomato sauce

Dredge squirrel pieces in seasoned flour and brown in olive oil. Add onion, pepper, and garlic. Sauté. Add oregano, mace, cloves, and wine.

Cover and simmer 20 minutes.

While the squirrel is simmering, in a separate pan, sauté mushrooms in butter. Add tomato sauce. When the tomato-mushroom sauce is hot, spoon it over the sautéed squirrel and serve immediately.

Creole Baked Squirrel

4 squirrels, cut up, seasoned with salt, pepper

2 packets dry onion soup mix

2-1/4 cups boiling water

1 pound chopped tomatoes, drained

1 small can (7 oz.)) whole kernel corn, drained

1-1/2 cups uncooked white rice

1 bell pepper, chopped

Place squirrel pieces in a buttered baking pan. Combine remaining ingredients and pour over squirrel and cover baking pan. Bake in 350° oven for 1-1/2 to 2 hours or until squirrel is tender.

Squirrel Casserole

4 cups squirrel - cooked, boned, cut up

1 pkg. dry stuffing mix

1 can cream of mushroom soup + 1 cup of water

1 can cream of chicken soup

1 stick butter cut up on top

Layer ingredients in casserole dish—squirrel meat, soup and water mixture, stuffing—with butter on top and cook 30 minutes at 350 degrees.

Baked Squirrel with Sherry Sauce

4 dressed squirrels, cut in pieces

8 cups water

1 tablespoon salt

2 teaspoons vinegar

1/3 cup all-purpose flour

Salt and pepper

2 tablespoons butter or margarine

2 tablespoons vegetable oil

8 oz. fresh whole mushrooms

Sherry Sauce

1 cup chicken broth

1/4 cup sherry

1 tablespoon Worcestershire sauce

1/4 teaspoon season salt

Dash of hot pepper sauce

Pre-heat oven to 350°. In a large non-metallic bowl combine squirrel pieces, water, 1 tablespoon salt and vinegar. Cover bowl and let stand at room temperature for 1 hour. Drain and discard liquid. Pat squirrel pieces dry and set aside. Combine flour, salt and pepper in a large plastic food storage bag and shake to mix. Add squirrel pieces and shake to coat. In a large cast iron skillet, melt the butter in the oil over medium-low heat. Add the coated squirrel pieces and brown on all sides over medium to medium-high heat. Transfer the squirrel pieces and pan drippings to a 3 quart casserole and add mushrooms. Combine ingredients for sherry sauce and pour over squirrel and mushrooms. Bake about 1-1/2 hours, until tender.

Squirrel Pot Pie

4 squirrels, quartered

1 can mixed vegetables, drained

1/3 cup Worcestershire sauce

1/3 stick of butter, melted

1 frozen pie crust

2-3 tablespoons Cajun-style seasoning

Put quartered squirrels in a crock pot and cover with water. Add the seasoning. Set the temperature to medium and cover. Cook for 6-8 hours.

Pre-heat oven to 350°

Remove the meat from the crock pot and let it cool until you can remove the meat from the bones without getting burned. In a mixing bowl combine the meat, the mixed vegetables, Worcestershire sauce and melted butter.

Spoon the mixture into the pie crust, add the top crust. Slit the top crust or poke some holes in it with a fork to allow steam to vent. Bake for about 30 minutes, or until crust is browned. Serve while hot.

Squirrel Pie

1 squirrel, cut up

3 tablespoons all-purpose flour

1/2 tablespoon chopped parsley

1 teaspoon salt

1/8 teaspoon pepper

1/2 cup raw mushrooms, cut up

2 cups milk

Biscuits:

2 cups all-purpose flour

4 teaspoons baking powder

1/2 teaspoon salt

1/4 cup vegetable shortening

2/3 cup milk

Cover squirrel pieces with water and simmer for about an hour. Remove meat from bones. Add flour, parsley, salt, pepper, and mushrooms to the meat stock. Bring mixture to a boil, then reduce heat and simmer until it thickens. Add meat and pour into baking dish.

Prepare the biscuit dough by sifting dry ingredients together. Cut in shortening and add milk a little at a time while stirring until dry ingredients are moistened. Roll the dough until it fits the baking dish. Cover the meat mixture with the dough and bake in 350° oven until crust is golden brown, about 35 minutes.

Squirrel and Dumplings

4-6 older squirrels

1 medium onion, chopped

1 stalk celery, chopped

1 can chicken broth, or 2-3 chicken bouillon cubes

2 tablespoons butter (unsalted, if using bouillon cubes)

Water to cover

Place skinned and cleaned squirrels in large pot. Add onion and celery. Add chicken broth and enough water to cover; or, cover with water and add chicken bouillon cubes. Cover pot and bring to boil over high heat. Reduce heat to medium and continue to boil until squirrels are fork tender, about 2 hours. Remove squirrels and pull meat from bones with a fork. Strain broth and set aside.

Dumplings: Mix 1-1/2 cups all-purpose flour, 1 egg, 1 cup of broth; continue adding flour until dough no longer sticks to the bowl and can be rolled. Roll dough out approximately 1/4-inch thick on floured surface; use knife to cut dough into strips approximately 2 inches wide and 3 inches long.

Return broth to large pot over high heat and bring to boil. Add squirrel meat, 1 can Cream of Mushroom soup and 1 cup of fresh, sliced mushrooms or 1 small can of mushrooms, drained. Add dumplings one at a time. Reduce heat to low and cook until dumplings are done. Season with salt and pepper to taste.

Barbecued Squirrel

Place any number of squirrels in a large enough pot to hold them and cover with water. Add salt and fresh ground pepper. Boil squirrels for 2 hours. Place squirrels, 1 cup of broth and 2-3 tablespoons of butter in a disposable aluminum foil roasting pan (or make your own disposable pan from a couple of sheets of heavy-duty aluminum foil). Lay a sheet of heavy duty foil over the pan and crimp edges to seal. Place the pan over a low charcoal fire or low heat on your gas grill.

After 45 minutes remove squirrels from the pan, place directly on barbecue grill and brush on your favorite barbecue sauce. Grill for about 15 minutes, turning once, or until sauce has caramelized the way you like it. Remove from grill and serve hot.

Squirrel Pate

Boil 6 older squirrels until tender, about 2 hours. In the last five minutes add 3 eggs in shells. Remove eggs and immerse immediately in cold water. Remove squirrels and let cool. Remove meat from the bones after squirrels are cool enough to handle, and peel the eggs. Using a food processor, grind meat and place in a bowl, then grind eggs and add to meat. Mix in enough mayonnaise for spreadable consistency, salt and fresh ground pepper to taste. Serve on toast or crackers with your favorite garnishes as a hors d'oeuvre.

Squirrel and Pasta Casserole

6-8 squirrels

2 chicken bouillon cubes

1 stalk celery, chopped

1 bay leaf

1 teaspoon fresh ground pepper

Pasta

2 tablespoons extra virgin olive oil

2 cans crushed tomatoes

1 can Ro-Tel brand tomatoes

2 small cans mushrooms, with liquid

1 clove garlic, crushed, chopped fine

Salt

Pepper

In a large pot, cover squirrels with water. Add chicken bouillon cubes, chopped celery, bay leaf, and pepper. Boil until squirrels are tender, about 2 hours. Strain and reserve about 2 quarts of the broth. In a large roasting pan brown spaghetti, linguini, penne pasta, or pasta shells (your choice) in olive oil, stirring often to avoid burning and sticking. Add crushed tomatoes, Ro-Tel brand tomatoes (diced tomatoes and green chili peppers), mushrooms with liquid, garlic, squirrel meat, broth, salt and fresh ground pepper.

Bake covered in 350° oven for 1-1/2 hours, stirring often. Sprinkle with grated parmesan cheese and shredded mozzarella cheese and return dish to the oven, uncovered, for 20-30 minutes, or until cheese is hot, bubbling and lightly browned.

•••

Made in the USA
Middletown, DE
17 August 2024

59304059R00068